THE UNIVERSAL
PRIMACY OF CHRIST

THE UNIVERSAL
PRIMACY OF CHRIST

by

Francis Xavier Pancheri, O.F.M.Conv.
S.T.D.

Translated and Adapted
by

Juniper B. Carol, O.F.M., S.T.D.

CHRISTENDOM PUBLICATIONS
Route 3, Box 87
Front Royal, Virginia 22630

ISBN: 0-931888-16-6
L.C. Classification No.: BT205.P25

A translation of the original essay: *Il Primato universale di Cristo*, by
Francesco Saverio Pancheri, O.F.M. Conv., contributed to the symposium
Problemi e figure della Scuola Scotistica del Santo (Padova, Edizioni Messag-
gero, 1966).

NIHIL OBSTAT:
Michael D. Meilach, O.F.M.
Censor deputatus

IMPRIMI POTEST
Very Rev. Alban A. Maguire, O.F.M.
Minister Provincial

IMPRIMATUR
W. Thomas Larkin, D. D.
Bishop of St. Petersburg, Fla.

CONTENTS

Abbreviations

AER   -American Ecclesiastical Review
Ang   -Angelicum
Ant   -Antonianum
AOFM   -Acta Ordinis Fratrum Minorum
APAR   -Acta Pontificiae Academiae Romanae S. Thomae Aq.
ASCSI   -Acta Secundi Congressus Scholastici Internationalis Oxonii et Edimburgi 11-17 sept. 1966 celebrati. Studia Scholastica-Scotistica
BT   -Bulletin Thomiste
BSFEM   -Bulletin de la Société Française d'Etudes Mariales
CdJ   -Cahiers de Joséphologie
CF   -Collectanea Franciscana
Crd   -The Cord
DTC   -Dictionnnaire de Théologie Catholique
Dvts   -Divinitas
EF   -Etudes Franciscaines
EHLD   -Etudes d'Histoire Littéraire et Doctrinale
EmR   -Ecumenical Review
ER   -Ecclesiastical Review
EstF   -Estudios Franciscanos
FEC   -Franciscan Educational Conference
FF   -La France Franciscaine
FS   -Franciscan Studies
HPR   -Homiletic and Pastoral Review
IER   -Irish Ecclesiastical Record
Int   -Interest
JTS   -Journal of Theological Studies
Ltm   -Laurentianum
MF   -Miscellanea Francescana
MSR   -Mélanges de Science Religieuse
PG   -Patrologia Graeca
PL   -Patrologia Latina
RPL   -Revue Philosophique de Louvain
RSPT   -Revue de Sciences Philosopiques et Théologiques
RTh   -Revue Thomiste
ScCatt   -La Scuola Cattolica
SF   -Studi Francescani
SPT   -Les Sciences Philosophiques et Théologiques
Spz   -Sapienza
WuW   -Wissenschaft und Weisheit

Preface

"The most harmful books are those that have an explanation for everything" (Voltaire). Assuming the French philosopher's dictum to be true, the book we are now presenting to our cultured readers is bound to do incalculable "harm." The reason is obvious. It so happens that, theologically speaking, the absolute and universal Primacy of Christ—the theme of this study—does embody the ultimate explanation of all things. More precisely: Christ's Primacy, as expounded and championed in this thoughtful disquisition, necessarily implies that Jesus Christ is the exemplary, meritorious and final cause, the *raison d'être* of absolutely everything which is not God. This Primacy, then, constitutes the only fully satisfactory explanation of any and everything which, in the vast realm of divine operations *ad extra*, has an explanation at all, whether in the natural or in the supernatural order.

Let us look at it this way. The most important thing in our lives is our religion. The most important facet of our religion is Christology. And the most important phase of Jesus Christ, as Man, is His unconditioned predestination, because that is precisely what constitutes Him, as Man, the very heart, center and foundation of the entire universe. It is only *in Him* that we discover the adequate answer to whatever questions may arise in any created mind concerning the purpose of creation and everything in it.

But why another book on a subject that has been so extensively and repeatedly ventilated in the past? The present essay has at least one unique feature which, in my considered judgment, amply justifies its publication. It offers, for the first time in the English language, a frank and objective analysis of the theological incongruities inherent in the traditional Scotistic theory to explain Christ's universal Primacy. At the same time, and follow-

9

ing some daring insights, the resourceful author has carried Scotus' luminous principles to their ultimate, logical—and surprising—conclusions. These conclusions, organized in a coherent and harmonious synthesis, spell out the definitive solution to a thorny problem that has left our theologians hopelessly divided through the course of the centuries. Obviously, an investigation of this nature is well deserving, if not of an *a priori* endorsement, at least of an unbiased examination.

The author of this volume, Fr. Francis Xavier Pancheri, O.F.M. Conv., is a distinguished Italian theologian, well known for his impressive doctoral dissertation on Matthias Joseph Scheeben and for his frequent contributions to the fields of Ecclesiology and Christology. Since graduating from Fribourg University, he has been engaged in a very fruitful apostolate: the theological training of future priests, mostly in Padua and in Rome. At present, he is President of the Pontifical Theological Faculty of the *Seraphicum* in the Eternal City.

It is only fair to inform our readers that this is not so much a translation as an adaptation and condensation of Fr. Pancheri's original essay. The adaptation, however, despite numerous stylistic alterations, has meticulously respected the author's thought, leaving it always intact. I have also taken the liberty to add here and there some bibliographical references which should be profitable to our English-speaking readers. For all the above, I have requested and obtained the author's gracious permission.

It is to be hoped that the present treatise, despite its somewhat technical presentation, will find a wide appeal not only in the restricted circle of professional theologians, but also in the broader area of discerning students craving to scale the lofty heights of the Christological mystery in order to deepen their appreciation of Jesus Christ's all-pervasive role in the universe.

Fr. Juniper B. Carol, O.F.M.
Feast of the Incarnation
March 25, 1983

Introduction

It is an easily established fact that the doctrine of Christ's universal primacy is inseparably associated with the name of the Scottish Franciscan John Duns Scotus (d. 1308). The theologians who drew their inspiration from the Subtle Doctor always made much of it, regarding it as a characteristic facet of his teaching, together with the "thesis" concerning Mary's Immaculate Conception. As a matter of fact, a profound nexus does bind the two doctrines. This attitude on the part of Scotus' followers was due not only to *esprit de corps* and loyalty to one's School, but also to a firm conviction that the Savior's absolute supremacy is clearly taught in divine Revelation and constitutes the very heart of Christianity.[1]

In this essay we will adopt a historico-doctrinal presentation as the most appropriate not only to appraise better the main thrust of Scotus' teaching, but also to grasp the contribution of his distinguished commentators who taught in Padua during the seventeenth century. Our investigation is limited to only a few of them in order not to extend our treatment unduly and also because it seems to us that the entire Scotistic "tradition" on the subject is adequately mirrored in those selected. The method chosen will make it possible for us to follow, step by step, the doctrine of the primacy .in its fundamental themes, from its uncertain and modest origins up to our own times when the Franciscan position, while not as yet enjoying a definitive formulation, nevertheless increasingly assumes the central and essential relevance it deserves.

Our treatment will be divided as follows:

Chapter I: *The Great Pioneers*, with particular mention of St. Anselm, Alexander of Hales, St. Bonaventure, and St. Thomas Aquinas.

Chapter II: *Blessed John Duns Scotus.*

Chapter III: *The Contribution of Theological Schools*, with special attention given to Cardinal Cajetan, the Salmanticenses, and Thomassin.

Chapter IV: *Súarez's Conciliatory Thesis.*

Chapter V: *The Scotistic School* with its different currents; St. Bernardine of Siena, St. Lawrence of Brindisi; M. J. Scheeben, K. Barth.

Chapter VI: *The Paduan Scotistic Theologians*, Fabbri, Belluti, Mastri.

Chapter VII: *Conclusions* concerning the theological, ecclesiological and anthropological problems.

1.
The Great Pioneers

The predominantly Christological outlook of many Greek Fathers and their concept of grace disposed them to a strong grasp of the fundamental role of Christ's supremacy. Indeed, their Christology was governed by the so-called "physical theory" of the Incarnation. The effect of Christ's mystery was recognized especially in the "divinization of man."[2] These basic principles, which have in St. Irenaeus, St. Athanasius, and St. Gregory of Nyssa their most authoritative defenders, paved the way to an open statement of the theology of Christ's primacy. The best known explicit representatives are St. Cyril of Alexandria (d. 444) and St. Maximus the Confessor (d. 662). The following text of St. Maximus embodies a perfect formulation of our doctrine.

[Christ] is that great and hidden mystery (Col. 1: 25). This is that blessed end [télos] for which all things were created. This is the divine scope foreknown before the beginning of creatures, which we define to be the end that was foreknown, on account of which all things [exist], but itself [exists] on account of nothing. With this end in view God produced the essences of creatures. This is properly the end of providence and of the things foreknown. . . . This is the mystery that contains all the ages and that manifests the great plan of God which is infinite and pre-existed the ages in an infinite manner. . . . Really, it was for the sake of Christ . . . that all the ages and the things in the ages themselves received the beginning and the end of existence in Christ. . . . This [hypostatic union] was made when Christ appeared in the last times. By itself it is the fulfillment of the foreknowledge of God.[3]

In the theology of the West, owing to a different perspective and different fundamental concerns, the problem of Christ's primacy began to be

13

formulated in an autonomous fashion and within the framework of Western predilection for the subject of sin and redemption. St. Anselm, as we shall see, imprinted here a precise and rigorous direction. The "Father of Scholasticism" was truly the notable starting point for the doctrine of the primacy in Latin theology and conditioned it profoundly. Beyond the different ways of stating the problem in general, we must note that in Latin theology the thesis assumed a hypothetical formulation expressed in the well-known query: "Whether the Son of God would have become incarnate if Adam had not sinned." The hamartiocentric mentality was, then, the clue to understanding every theological problem, including that of Christ's primacy. In brief, the primary concern was to establish the connection between the sin to be repaired and Christ as the Redeemer.

With this premise in mind, it was asked: Is Christ's redemptive function pre-eminent to the extent that it absorbs every other "end" of the Incarnation? Among the various concrete "motives" of the Incarnation, which is the primary and subordinating one? Is it our redemption from sin? If this be the decisive motive—as seems evident from Sacred Scripture—would Christ have existed if Adam hadn't sinned?

Note how the step is taken from the hamartiocentric mentality to the hypothetical formulation of the question. But it is clear that the answer is already included in the general premise that leads to the hypotheical formulation. Hamartiocentrism cannot but arrive at the conclusion that God would not have become incarnate if Adam's offense had not intervened, since its point of departure is the presupposition that the dominating motive or end of Christ's coming is precisely our redemption from sin. The manner of presenting the problem became so common and obvious that it was adopted even by those who gave a different answer to the question; for these, the hypothetical formula will be only an embarrassing nuisance. It is this hamartiocentrism that obstructed, for centuries, a true knowledge of Christ's primacy, making of it a small appendix to the doctrine of redemption instead of the heart of the Christian salvation mystery.

1. St. Anselm of Canterbury (d. 1109): His Decisive Influence

The very first treatise dealing specifically with the world's redemption is St. Anselm's *Cur Deus Homo*, written at the beginning of the twelfth century. Its suggestive title already declares with precision the topic relative to the end of the Incarnation.

The theory of satisfaction which dominates the celebrated Anselmian opus became one of the stable facets of the entire Scholastic period and continued, through post-Tridentine theology, to make its weight felt up to the present time.[4]

Regarding the world's redemption, St. Anselm's thought rests on two fundamental points: a) the notion that God is man's wisest and most just sovereign Lord; and b) the universal fact of original sin, source of every other personal guilt, which places man in a state of spiritual death, although leaving everyone with the obligation of possessing original justice. That is to say, sinful man retains the destination to the supernatural end to which God has ṛaised the entire human race. Having established these two points, which are taught by Revelation without any shadow of doubt, Anselm wishes to prove with "necessary" reasons,[5] not only the fittingness but also the necessity of the Incarnation and of the death on the Cross. The basic coloration, then, of the *Cur Deus Homo* is eminently hamartiocentric and anthropocentric. Besides, the concept of redemption is dominated by the notions of justice, rights and duties, punishment and satisfaction.

St. Anselm notes that sin is a "quasi-infinite" offense against God; it defrauds Him of His rights and of the honor which is His due. This is so because an offense is measured by the person offended and not by the offending person. Since God is an infinite Person, sin involves a guilt, a "theft" of unlimited gravity. The offense given to God by sin cannot go unpunished; it demands a satisfaction and a proportionate punishment.[6]

This "logic" is dictated by the demands of divine justice. Appealing to divine goodness, one could think of divine forgiveness; but since goodness does not operate without justice, simple forgiveness is impossible; that would be equivalent to placing the just and the unjust on the same level.

On the other hand, punishment is not the solution. That would mean that the whole human race should be condemned to Hell, which is precisely the proportionate punishment. In that case, the divine plan of salvation would be totally frustrated since no one would be saved. The divine plan must be carried out notwithstanding man's deficiencies, for God is faithful and infallible. Having, therefore, excluded the first alternative from the dilemma "either punishment or porportionate satisfaction," the only remaining solution is the latter.[7]

But who can make satisfaction for sin? Not man, because "it is impossible for a sinner to satisfy for a sinner."[8] Neither a sinless man, nor a pure creature, nor even an angel could do it. To satisfy means giving to God something which is not due to Him by another title. Now, everything the creature is and has is owed entirely to God as Creator. Furthermore, the eventual reparation offered by a creature would always be of finite value, while the gravity of sin is infinite.[9]

From the above it follows that the dramatic situation comes down to this: Only God can supply an adequate reparation. And yet, since the human race is guilty, it cannot remain extraneous to the reparation. God, as God, cannot make satisfaction to Himself; that would be pure fiction. It is necessary, therefore, to have a God-Man, Jesus Christ, so as to render possible a true satisfaction which is in harmony with all the demands involved. But does it not follow from all this that man forces God to wish the Incarnation? No, Anslem answers. Since God freely created man and freely raised him to a supernatural destiny, it is from His own salvific will that the necessity of the Incarnation arises.[10]

Another angle must be considered. Through which acts could Christ make satisfaction for sin? Surely not through those that were due to the Father by other titles, such as acts of obedience, love and adoration. There remains only one possibility: voluntary death. Since the Savior was absolutely free from sin, he was not subject to the law of death. Freely accepting the death on the Cross, He truly satisfies through a free act which is not otherwise due to God, and the satisfaction offered has an infinite value, coming as it does from the infinite Person of the God-Man.[11]

It is thus that St. Anselm reaches the conclusion that the Incarnation and the death on the Cross were "necessary." As mentioned before, the Anselmian terminology and perspective, together with the various notions integrating his thesis, have played a decisive role in Western theology in all that concerns the relationship between Christ and sin.[12] Anthropocentrism and hamartiocentrism have in him an outstanding representative. His followers' position will be, briefly: Condign satisfaction for sin is the precise and adequate cause of the Incarnation.

May it be said, then, that St. Anselm is faithful to the Fathers' heritage and to the teaching of Sacred Scripture? Let us bear in mind that St. Anselm presents the Incarnation as being demanded by the rights of divine justice. Sacred Scripture, on the contrary, shows us that it is divine goodness that takes the initiative relative to the decree of the mystery. It is as a consequence of this gift that Christ renders all glory to God. And of course, according to Scripture, there is no opposition whatever among the divine attributes on account of sin. As M. Richard has put it:

> But in order to elucidate this, it was necessary to show, first of all, that the redemption is the initiative of Love which gives and forgives. This is not sufficiently emphasized by St. Anselm.[13]

The gravest defect of the Anselmian perspective is the total neglect of the value of the Incarnation as a mystery of universal divinization, according to the admirable teaching of the Greek Fathers. Latin juridicism, already present in Tertullian and St. Augustine, acquires in Anselm an absolute importance and is colored by Germanic justice, according to which an offended nobleman *had* to demand an adequate satisfaction, not from just anybody, but from one of his peers. Indeed, in the Anselmian thought redemption appears situated within a cold, abstract sphere of debit and credit, within a rigid scheme of "injured honor," and "adequate satisfaction." We seem to be dealing here with a mechanical world of moral-juridical values; all personal intimacy seems to have vanished. Thus according to G. Oggioni:

> The great limitation of Anselm's theory is not what he has said, but what he has passed over in silence. Indeed, too little has he spoken about grace, about God's love as the root of Christ's redemptive work, and about sanctifying grace as its final result.[14]

One may measure the distance which separates St. Anselm's theology from that of the Fathers, especially the Greek, if one compares it with the teaching of one of the greatest among them—St. Cyril of Alexandria.

For the prominent Alexandrian, who was the echo of a vast tradition, the Incarnation is "the beginning of God's ways." Jesus Christ is the foundation of every created reality. He was willed by God before the foundation of the world as the principle of our elevation to the supernatural order. His divinizing power is such that rational creatures, being subject to the test of finite freedom and having fallen into sin, find in the pre-existing and unmovable foundation which is Christ, the beginning of their resurrection, without any change having been introduced by sin in the original plan of God's goodness.[15]

2. Alexander of Hales, O.F.M. (d. 1245)

For all its wide diffusion, St. Anselm's position was not the only one known in the early Middle Ages. There are other voices which present our subject in a different manner. Among these, Rupert of Deutz, O.S.B. (d. 1135) deserves to be mentioned. The author's doctrine is not systematic. His thought on this question is rather fragmentary and not always uniform. On the whole, however, the following general presentation emerges clearly: God created the world for the love and glory of Christ, in order to prepare for Him a royal palace and a court. The Word became man in order to have brethren whose firstborn He would be. The Incarnation was willed independently of Adam's sin and "prior" to it. Men and angels were created in view of the future God-Man, who is the exemplary cause of all creation.[16]

This theme, which was present also in other theologians of the early

Middle Ages, [17] finds some illustrious proponents among the great Scholastics of the thirteenth century. The first is Alexander of Hales.[18] His merit in this matter is that he treats it in a systematic fashion. His arguments to show that the Incarnation was decreed independently of the Fall are varied. The primary is that based on the well-known principle, "Bonum est diffusivum sui," an argument which is fundamental in Platonic and Neo-platonic thought to explain the existence of the universe. Alexander reminds us that God is the "summum Bonum." The "diffusio" of this goodness takes place first *ad intra* and produces the divine Persons. But this does not exhaust the whole possibility implied in the principle, since a "diffusio ad extra" is still possible.

> Si ergo ejus debet esse summa diffusio, quia est summum Bonum, convenientius est quod se diffundat in creatura; sed haec diffusio non potest intelligi summa nisi ipse uniatur creaturae; ergo convenit quod Deus uniatur creaturae, et maxime humanae, sicut ostensum est. Ergo, posito quod ipsa non esset lapsa, adhuc ei uniretur summum Bonum.[19]

It is clear that we are dealing here with an *a priori* argument based on the divine nature itself; God, being "summum Bonum," must communicate Himself "summe" also *ad extra*.[20]

Another argument, used to answer an objection from the Liturgy (i.e., the well-known *felix culpa*), is of a positive character. Sacred Scripture hints that Lucifer and his angels fell because they refused to accept Christ, the future God-Man, as the source of their own supernatural life. Therefore, the Incarnation precedes the prevision of sin.[21] Besides, as St. Augustine teaches, God became man in order to be the supernatural life of men, and therefore, "concedendum est quod etiamsi non fuisset humana natura lapsa, adhuc est convenientia ad Incarnationem."[22] Note that the author does not speak of *rationes necessariae*, but only *ex convenientia*, and that he has openly abandoned the hamartiocentric perspective of St. Anselm.

It must be pointed out, however, that Alexander's principal arguments are based not on Scripture, but on *a priori* considerations of the divine nature. That is to say, the fact of the Incarnation is motivated, not starting from salvation history and hence from divine *freedom*, but rather directly from the divine nature itself and its attributes (wisdom, omnipotence, communicability). This is the radical defect and weakness of the argumentation—to wish to deduce immediately from the divine nature an event or a reality which depends solely on God's *free* will. In this respect. Alexander's *Summa* follows St. Anselm who, given the fact of sin, directly deduced the *necessity* of condign satisfaction from the divine attributes.

Speaking of Christ's predestination, Alexander admits that Christ is the cause of the predestination of all others,[23] but, unlike Scotus, he makes no use whatever of this argument in order to bolster his thesis. When the author considers the Incarnation in its relation to the universe, he again has recourse to *a priori* motives. For instance, the *Summa* seems to regard the Incarnation as the perfection of the universe, as its zenith and hence, in a certain sense, as deducible from the valuation of the universe itself. This view, besides being aprioristic, is totally wrong because it subordinates Christ to the world. The aprioristic method, as used in this case, is even less convincing; to say that the world demands the incarnation as its zenith is equivalent to denying the supernatural. Christ is not the "crown" of the universe. He is its foundation, its source, its end and scope—which is quite different.

We have deemed it opportune to recall the theological reasoning of Alexander's *Summa* because it was rejected by later theologians who defend an Incarnation independent of sin, and also because many adversaries of this thesis frequently referred to Alexander's arguments as if they were the only "proofs" of the Scotistic theory.

3. St. Bonaventure (d. 1274)

Of all the great scholars of the Middle Ages, the Seraphic Doctor is the one who accords our subject the greatest amplitude and the most complete analysis. It is important that we pay close attention to his teaching because of his influence on those who subordinate the Incarnation to the prevision of the Fall.

St. Bonaventure introduces the problem by treating of the *congruitas* of the Incarnation.[24] This fittingness is studied especially *ex parte Dei*. He shows how this mystery brings out in a marvelous way the divine power, wisdom and goodness. The motivation of fittingness is analyzed in various ways:

1) God's infinite power, wisdom and goodness should be manifested in a perfect manner. This takes place only through Christ who is the "effectus aliquo modo infinitus."

2) The perfection of the order of the universe. In the series of beings, the first should join the last. It was fitting, then, that the divine Word should be united to man.

3) In God there are three divine Persons in only one nature. It was fitting that there should be also a divine Person in more than one nature.

4) God is the infinite remunerator. It was fitting that He should render

man blessed according to his whole nature—soul and body. The external
senses of the body can be rendered blessed only through a corporeal vision
of the glorious God-Man.

5) In order to overcome the infirmity of man's sin it was necessary to
have a God-Man as Mediator. Therefore, "videtur quod opus Incarnationis
maxime congruum fuit pietati divinae."[25]

The reader will have noted that St. Bonaventure mentions all the
arguments of Alexander's *Summa* plus a few of his own. But the Seraphic
Doctor repeatedly stresses that he is reflecting on the Incarnation as an already
known event. He is not dealing with *a priori* deductions. The argument from
fittingness is never a demonstration, as some of his predecessors seemed
to think.

4. The "Ratio Praecipua Incarnationis"

Having thus freed the field of all equivocal interference, the Seraphic
Doctor enters the heart of the problem: What is the *interior* reason of the
Incarnation? Observe that the *extrinsic* finality is not under discussion. God,
author of the Incarnation, is always guided in His actions by His most wise
will to share and to manifest His glory; hence, the final end of His actions
can be none other than He Himself.[26]

Furthermore, it is not a question of proving the possibility of the Incarnation in this or that hypothesis. The question centers on the Incarnation
as it was willed by God in the present economy of salvation. Even if
hypothetical *expressions* occur, St. Bonaventure never means to refer to
hypothetical *facts*.

The capital question, then, is as follows: What is the fundamental meaning and purpose of the Incarnation in the present order of salvation? What
is its *ratio praecipua*? Note the excellent choice of terminology. St. Bonaventure does not inquire into the *motive* of the Incarnation, but rather into its
ratio. The former term designates something which moves someone from
the outside, and God cannot be "moved" by anything or anyone but Himself.
The latter term ("ratio"), on the contrary, wishes to specify the interior
meaning, the intrinsic principle of intelligibility, i.e., that which primarily
determines all other components.

The Seraphic Doctor answers his own question by appealing, first of
all, to the authority of theologians: "Circa hoc duplex est magistrorum
opinio." This shows that at that time there were precisely two *opinions* on
the subject, and hence each was recognized as probable. Before presenting
his own viewpoint, he gives an exact and accurate exposition of the two
positions so that his readers may assess the intrinsic value and the cogency

of the arguments.

The proponents of the first opinion make a distinction between the substance of the Incarnation and the passible modality of its concrete execution. Having made this distinction, they affirm: The "ratio praecipua" of the substance of the Incarnation, the fundamental meaning of the mystery

> est multiplex perfectio surgens ex dignitate illius operis. Incarnatio enim facit ad perfectionem hominis et per consequens ad perfectionem totius unversi, in hoc quod complet et completionem dat humano generi, secundum illud quod respicit naturam et secundum illud quod respicit gratiam et secundum quod respicit gloriam.[27]

All this can be brought about by the Incarnation regardless of the moral condition of mankind (i.e., with or without original sin).

Nevertheless, in its concrete execution, the Incarnation did assume the modality of passibility and mortality. Now, the "ratio praecipua" of this passibility is the redemption from sin. Hence, only the passibility, and not the substance of the Incarnation, follows the prevision of original sin.[28]

In favor of this first opinion St. Bonaventure lines up—one might say, enthusiastically—a long series of arguments in the *Sed contra* which introduces the discussion. They are based on the divine attributes, on the consideration of man and the universe, and also on the untenable consequences of the second opinion. In order to avoid repetition, we shall mention them when we examine the Doctor's answer to them.

The second opinion holds that the "praecipua ratio Incarnationis est reparatio generis humani, quamvis aliae multae sint rationes congruentiae huic adnexae." This is so much so that "nisi genus humanum fuisset lapsum, Verbum Dei non fuisset incarnatum." There is no distinction between the substance and the modality of the Incarnation. Both were oriented to the redemption; hence, the Incarnation was willed by God "after" the prevision of the Fall.

Before proceeding to give the reasons for this second opinion, the Seraphic Doctor expresses a basic judgment as follows:

> Quis autem horum modorum dicendi [i.e., the two opinions] verior sit, novit Ille qui pro nobis incarnari dignatus est. Quis autem horum alteri praeponendus sit, difficile est videre, pro eo quod uterque modus catholicus est et a viris catholicis sustinetur. Uterque etiam modus excitat animam ad devotionem, secundum diversas considerationes.[29]

Nevertheless, of the two opinions, he decidedly chooses the second. This would seem an unjustified choice, considering everything he has said. And yet, it is not, for a general motive intervenes in favor of the second: "Videtur autem primus modus magis consonare judicio rationis, secundus tamen, ut apparet, plus consonat pietati fidei."

The reason for the last statement is that the second opinion harmonizes better with the teaching of Sacred Scripture and the Fathers of the Church.[30] As an argument *ex ratione theologica*, he points out that the primary motivations of the first opinion are based, ultimately, on a subordination of Christ to the universe. Indeed, if the Incarnation is demanded by the perfection of the universe, then it follows that "quodam modo Deum infra perfectionem universi concludit et quamdam necessitatem Incarnationis ponit Ei, cum dicit opera ejus aliter ad perfectionem non perduci."

But the mystery of the Incarnation is beyond all the demands of creatures; it is an absolutely gratuitous work of God's love. That is why the second opinion, which stresses this basic reality, is more in conformity with piety. This is, according to St. Bonaventure, the capital and decisive objection against the first opinion.

The other reasons are of less weight. For example, according to the second opinion, the mystery of the Incarnation is so great that "non debuit fieri nisi ex maxima causa." This cause can be found neither in man nor in the universe, but only in God, that is, "propter placandam divinam iram et restauranda omnia." Finally, the affection of the faithful is inflamed more by the thought that God became Incarnate to destroy the sin of man than by the thought that He became man in order to bring to perfection the work He had already begun. Hence, the second opinion is to be preferred because "plus consonat pietati fidei, Deum magis honorificat, Incarnationis mysterium magis commendat, et affectum nostrum ardentius inflammat."[31]

With these premises in mind, St. Bonaventure now undertakes a rebuttal of the arguments in favor of the first opinion.

The first four are not very cogent because they hinge aprioristically on creatures' need for the Incarnation, and we know this mystery is absolutely gratuitous. The Seraphic Doctor has an easy task showing this weakness. The other five arguments are of a different order; they are based on Christ's pre-eminence in the present order of salvation. The fifth states: If the redemption is the *ratio praecipua* of the Incarnation, Christ appears to be an *opus occasionatum*, which is absurd. The sixth stresses even more this absurdity by noting that if man's malice and guilt be the primary cause of the Incarnation, then "videtur quod homo reportet commodum de malitia."

The seventh and eighth arguments start out from the fact that, in the present order of things, Christ is the Head of the Church, not only as God but also as Man. Since the order of salvation is historically only one, it follows that the Christ-Head is willed by God "before" the prevision of sin. Furthermore, matrimony, by divine institution (Eph. 5:32), "significat conjunctionem Christi cum Ecclesia." But matrimony was established "before" the prevision of sin. Therfore, so was Jesus Christ.[32]

In answering the above arguments, St. Bonaventure is no longer at ease. Concerning the *occasionality* of Christ's predestination, he observes: It is not true that in the second opinion Christ was predestined *occasionaliter*, since God *freely* willed Christ after the prevision of sin. Having created man, and having foreseen the fall and willed its redemption, "ideo fecit [eum] quia se reparaturum cognovit; et ideo principalius in intentione fuit reparatio lapsi quam conditio ejus ad lapsum possibilis." Frankly, the answer is far from satisfactory. The shifting from the order of execution to the order of intention, as we see it in the answer, does not solve anything. What we are trying to do is precisely to determine whether in the order of intention in the present divine plan, Christ's predestination is or is not dependent on the prevision of sin and hence occasioned by it. The Doctor says that God foresees man and his sin, and wills its reparation in Christ. That means that Christ is willed "after" the prevision of sin and occasioned by it.[33]

Equally unsatisfactory is the answer to the argument based on Christ as Head of the Church. In this connection, St. Bonaventure deduces all the consequences that are implicit in the position he holds. He openly affirms that there are *two* orders of salvation: one, prior to sin, whose head is God directly and the Word as God; then a second order after sin, having the God-Man as head. The angels, therefore, are not members of the Mystical Body of Christ.[34]

But is this solution in harmony with Revelation? May one hold that there are two orders of salvation? Isn't Jesus Christ the only Mediator of all? Of course, the "logic" of the opinion endorsed by the Saint necessarily demands the affirmation of two orders of salvation. But should not this conclusion (which is out of harmony with Revelation) throw some light on the fragility and untenability of the premises whence it follows? In any case, St. Bonaventure, having set down the principle, loyally draws all the consequences.

The same observations are in order concerning the typological meaning of matrimony. St. Bonaventure informs us that matrimony has two meanings: " . . . significat enim conjunctionem *Dei* cum Ecclesia secundum caritatem, et significat etiam conjunctionem secundum unionem in personae unitate."

The first—*secundum caritatem*—would have existed even if man had not sinned, while the second pertains to the present order of salvation. But does not St. Paul state explicitly that the matrimony of innocent Adam was a symbol of Christ's unity with His Church? In order to evade the force of the argument, St. Bonaventure is always forced to speak of two orders of salvation. This is simply untenable, although it follows necessarily from his premises.

5. Observations

It is undeniable that the Seraphic Doctor has examined our question with the greatest care, with amplitude of perspective, and with every nuance possible. Nevertheless, he does not appear to regard the problem as bearing on the entire horizon of the theological discipline; it remains "a problem," although a very important and non-marginal one.

In order to gauge adequately the paramount value which St. Bonaventure attaches to Christ's primacy in his theology, the reader must turn his attention to the "Quaestiones Disputatae" *De scientia Christi, De perfectione evangelica*, the justly famous sermon entitled *Christus omnium Magister*, and the "Collationes" *De decem praeceptis, De septem donis*, and *In Hexaëmeron*.[35] In these writings Jesus Christ is forcefully portrayed as the principle of all knowledge and the source of all life. Bonaventurian theology is decidedly Christocentric in its structure. This, however, is hardly compatible with the *ratio praecipua* which he assigns to the Incarnation.

A second observation concerns the manner of formulating the question. In this respect, too, St. Bonaventure improves on his predecessors. He distinguishes well between the compass of fittingness (arising from the consideration of the Incarnation's relation to God and man) and that of the *ratio praecipua* which is intrinsic to the mystery itself in the complete order of salvation. This is precisely where the true difficulty lies. Since the Incarnation is an *opus ad extra* and therefore dependent on God's free will, we will not be able to discover its *ratio praecipua* by analyzing the nature and essential attributes of God, but only by considering the plan of salvation as manifested to us through supernatural Revelation. St. Bonaventure's progress in this respect marks a step forward in the study of this question.

6. The Argument "ex pietate"

As already noted, St. Bonaventure's choice of the second opinion is dictated by his reading of the sources of Revelation. As he puts it, the second viewpoint in question "magis consonat pietati fidei" and hence must be preferred to the first which "videtur magis consonare judicio rationis."

The reasoning *ex pietate* thus seems decisive in his solution. As a matter of fact, this type of argument is frequently used by the Seraphic Doctor.

J.G. Bourgerol, O.F.M. defines it as follows: "Of two theological propositions, one of which is theoretically closer to the truth, and the other is practically more religious, the latter is more likely and hence to be followed."[36]
This is a necessary sequel of the very concept of theology as understood
by the Doctor. The "pietas" toward God has here a fundamental function
to fulfill; it is faith lived.[37]

Concerning the first opinion, Bonaventure does not condemn its distinction between the substance and the modality of the Incarnation. He admits
that this opinion is more "subtle" than the second, more "logical," more
in conformity with reason. Nevertheless, he grasps with admirable precision the weakness of some of the theological arguments adduced by previous
authors in favor of the first opinion, especially the one which conceives of
Christ as the perfection of the universe. This, the holy Doctor points out,
is equivalent to subordinating Christ to creatures, which is exactly the conclusion these authors meant to discard in the first place and at all costs.
Bonaventure's evaluation here is supremely valid.

The same cannot be said of the holy Doctor's observations on the
arguments which the first opinion draws from the very concept of Christ's
primacy. In this respect, one senses that Bonaventure is endeavoring to avoid
outright the anthropocentrism and hamartiocentrism inherent in his personal
opinion. He does not succeed, of course. His answers are not persuasive.

In conclusion, we may point out that eventually the second opinion would
be known as "Thomistic." It seems to us, however, that it would be more
fitting to call it "Bonaventurian," at least if that appellation refers to its
origin and to the author who propounded it most fully.

7. St. Thomas Aquinas (d. 1274)

The Angelic Doctor discussed our topic in several of his works written
at various times through the years of his theological activity. With the exception of some nuances here and there, his thought on our subject remained always the same.[38] The problem, however, is treated not so much under
the aspect of Christ's primacy as that of the Incarnation's relationship to
the redemption along the well-known Anselmian lines.

The first thing to be noted is the manner of presenting the question.
Whereas St. Bonaventure endeavored to search for the *ratio praecipua* of
the Incarnation, St. Thomas always used the hypothetical "Utrum si homo
non peccasset, Deus incarnatus fuisset"—the formula which later became
standard. The difference is not only superficial with reference to Bonaventure; it actually reveals a direct dependence on St. Anselm's *Cur Deus Homo*.

Although St. Thomas constantly adopted the hypothetical formulation, it is clear that he did not mean to examine a pure hypothesis, an abstract possibility; he wished to elucidate a factual reality. It is nevertheless opportune to recall the difference of approach because sometimes we find statements made in this conneciton which do not correspond to the truth. Some, for example, emphasize that while the Angelic Doctor always moved in the concrete field of reality, the "others" have toyed with the unreal and trifled with hypotheses.[39] It was precisely owing to the authority of St. Thomas that the hypothetical formulation of the question prevailed everywhere. It is true, of course, that in adopting this manner of speaking, the Angelic Doctor was merely summing up what had already been expressed in *some* patristic texts.[40] For instance, in one of his sermons St. Augustine writes: "Si homo non perisset, Filius hominis non venisset."[41] St. Thomas knew this text and quoted it verbatim in his *Summa*.

8. The "Opinio praeferenda"

Concerning the solution of the question, we note that it coincides with that of St. Bonaventure, from whom St. Thomas borrowed the motivations as well. But St. Thomas adhered to it with less enthusiasm. He is more cautious and—one is tempted to say—less convinced than his Franciscan colleague.

Thus, in his *Commentary on the Sentences*, the Angelic Doctor reveals his thought with the same somewhat skeptical statement previously used by Bonaventure: "Respondeo dicendum quod hujus quaestionis veritatem solus ille scire potest qui natus est et oblatus quia ipse voluit."[42] Nevertheless, the authority of Scripture and of the Church Fathers induces him to affirm as "convenientius" that the Word would not have become incarnate if man had not sinned.

We find the same position in the *Summa Theologica*. After referring to the two opinions, the Saint tells us that "magis videtur assentiendum" to that viewpoint of those who hold that God would not have become man if Adam had remained faithful.[43] The main reason for this preference is the teaching of Sacred Scripture. Only Revelation can make known to us those truths that are beyond every natural exigency and which depend on the free will of God. Now, "cum in sacra Scriptura ubique Incarnationis ratio ex peccato primi hominis assignetur, *convenientius* dicitur Incarnationis opus ordinatum esse a Deo in remedium peccati, ita quod, peccato non existente, Incarnatio non fuisset." This is said concerning the present order of things. It is granted that abstractly God could have become man even if the state of original innocence had lasted.[44]

Concerning the arguments in favor of the first opinion, St. Thomas mentions some of them in connection with the fittingness of the Incarnation (e.g., it is fitting that God manifest visibly the invisible mysteries of Divine Life; God is the supreme Goodness: it was fitting for Him to communicate Himself *ad extra* in a perfect way); other arguments are examined in the article of the *Summa* which specifically discusses the concrete motive of the Incarnation. It is a question of motives based on the *capacity* of human nature, and here St. Thomas, like St. Bonaventure before him, has an easy task showing that the Incarnation can in no way be deduced from the requirements of human nature itself. Less convincing, however, is the Saint's answer to the argument based on Christ's predestination.[45] At any rate, the Angelic Doctor does not attach any decisive weight to this reasoning; it is more a consequence than a point of departure. We may note also that, for him, the question at hand is not particularly momentous for Christology, and much less for theology as a whole. He regards it as a marginal problem.

In the *Commentary on the Sentences* his solution is even more nuanced. Having presented the arguments in favor of the second opinion (the same as those mentioned later in the *Summa*) he adds:

> Alii vero dicunt quod cum per incarnationem Filii Dei non solum liberatio a peccato, sed etiam humanae naturae exaltatio et totius universi consummatio facta sit, etiam peccato non existente, propter has causas incarnatio fuisset; et hoc probabiliter sustineri potest.[46]

Briefly stated, St. Thomas *leaned* to the second opinion to which "magis assentiendum videtur" because of the teaching of Scripture and the Fathers; he did not adhere to it as decisively as St. Bonaventure did. For this reason it is necessary "to draw a sharply marked line of separation between St. Thomas and the Thomists," as Risi suggests.[47] Indeed, later Thomism holds that the *only valid* thesis is the one which subordinates the existence of Christ to the Fall of man. This is proclaimed as the *only* viewpoint which is in conformity with Revelation. Yet, the opinion which St. Thomas preferred was always for him an "opinio probabilior, convenientior," not a theological certainty.[48]

Furthermore, in order to grasp the mind of St. Thomas regarding our question, it must be remembered that for him the grace of the angels and of innocent Adam depended on Christ in an essential manner, and not only accidentally, as many Thomists claim.[49] According to the holy Doctor, angels and men belong to the Mystical Body of Christ. Hence, Christ is the Head of all *sensu univoco*. That means that the predestination of all follows that of Christ and depends on it. The evident conclusion should be that Christ was predestined "before" the prevision of sin and independently of it. But

St. Thomas never drew this conclusion which would have rendered untenable the second opinion, which he believed to be more probable. Why?

In the first place, because the argument based on predestination was never elaborated by the Angelic Doctor in this connection as a determining factor. In the second place—and this seems to be the main reason—because he conceived ontological finality as more a physical than a metaphysical ordination. The examples he uses to illustrate his thought are always of the physical order.[50] It follows that finality maintains a quasi-extrinsic relationship to the being whose end it is. For this reason God can modify the end of a being or of the universe without their changing their nature. In this physicist concept of finality it does not seem impossible or contradictory for God to have changed our supernatural end after the Fall. That is to say, while there was first an order of grace which did not include Christ, after the Fall such an order had its end in Christ, without any substantial modification having intervened.

In our considered judgment, this is a point of the greatest importance in the endeavor to understand the succession of the two supernatural orders already mentioned by St. Bonaventure and destined to become traditional within the Thomistic School. The point does not ordinarily receive the attention it deserves. As we shall see, John Duns Scotus, with a lucidity equal to his metaphysical insight, revealed the untenable equivocation inherent in the physicist concept of finality. This is why the argument based on predestination had for Scotus the decisive importance it did not have for Bonaventure or Thomas.[51]

9. The Plan of the Summa

A consideration of the general structure of the *Summa* discloses St. Thomas' position on our subject more graphically even than a reading of the texts that treat the question *ex professo*. In recent years the *Summa*'s plan, not so much from the historico-literary aspect, but from the thematic methodological viewpoint, has been the object of wide attention.[52] And not without good reason. After all, the redactional criterion used in the *Summa* is the indispensable key to the global intelligibility of Aquinas' thought and to his over-all vision of theology. The leading scholars who have done outstanding research along these lines are especially M. D. Chenu, O.P.,[53] A. Hayen, O.P.,[54] and E. Persson.[55] The salient results of their investigation may be summarized as follows:

The *ordo disciplinae* chosen by St. Thomas is due to the arrangement of theology according to the Aristotelian concept of science. It is well known that for Aristotle science, especially philosophy, is the knowledge of reality *per altissimas causas* according to the fourfold aspect of causality: efficient, final, material and formal. Science is thus knowledge that has the mark of universality and necessity. It is in this Aristotelian framework that St. Thomas introduces the Neoplatonic principle of the creature's *exitus* and *reditus* in relation to God. And it is in view of these premises that the various parts of the *Summa* are arranged and connected among themselves by the logical order resulting from such premises. The difficulty with this systematization concerns precisely the peculiar character of salvation history which, being a contingent, gratuitous and free work of God, lacks all necessity. In effect, St. Thomas introduces Christ at the end of his work (the *Tertia Pars*), after the entire theology, including even the tract on the supernatural order, has already been fully constructed.

According to the internal logical order of the *Summa*, after the treatment of God in Himself as the efficient-final cause, we have the tract on creation (i.e., the natural order), then on grace (the supernatural order), and finally Christ as the *via* for the *reditus in Deum*. (Note that this *reditus* is already essentially due to creatures inasmuch as they have been raised to the supernatural order.) According to this plan of *exitus—reditus*, the Incarnation emerges as a *means* to bring about the *reditus* which man had found impossible to achieve on account of Adam's disobedience.

What we have here is actually a succession of three plans: the universal one of creation; the particular one of grace which presupposes the first; and finally, the hypostatic order which presupposes both.[56] The *Summa* thus gives us a theology of creation and of the supernatural order antecedently to the appearance of Christ and abstracting from Him. Christ is projected, then, as a concrete *modality* of the creature's *reditus in Deum*. It is in this global vision that we can discover St. Thomas' compelling reason for regarding the Incarnation as having been conditioned by man's sin. In the over-all plan of the *Summa*, Christology is not central; it is rather an "addition" to a reality that has already been fully established in itself according to universal, necessary, metaphysical principles. In this persepctive, Christ was not constituted Head of the universe in the original plan of God; He *becomes* that in the course of history. He is somehow superimposed on the already existing reality of grace understood as the friendhsip of God, which from *gratia Dei* becomes *gratia Christi*. It is not, therefore, by mere chance, as Persson observes, that Christology is situated where it is in St. Thomas' principal work. On the contrary, it is a natural and necessary consequence of the work's basic structure.[57]

We hardly need to remark that this view of Christ's role has given rise to extremely grave objections. Does this elaboration really express the teaching of Sacred Scripture concerning Christ and His universal primacy? Can we calmly accept the statement that Jesus Christ is only the path of our *return* to God—or better: one modality of that return—instead of also the very reason for our *exitus a Deo?* As to the basic Thomistic assertion that Christ is only a *means*, how does one harmonize that with what Sacred Scripture teaches about the fundamental function of Christ as Head of all creation; that Christ is the one "in whom [God] has predestined us before the foundation of the world" (Eph. 1:4), and in whom "all things were made in heaven and on earth" in such a way that "He is before all things and everything subsists in Him" (Col. 1:16-17)?

Again: are we to believe that Christ is only a "redemptive modality" inserted into the pre-existing supernatural order? Must we not believe, on the contrary, that our election and adoption as sons are realities which derive totally from Christ? Does not this whole view prove the impossibility of forcing the biblical notion of salvation history into the Greek mold of a "metaphysica salutis"?

Prof. E. Gilson, reviewing Father Chenu's study—which showed this to be the true plan of the *Summa*—fully accepts its premises and conclusions. Those who wish to be Thomists *must* embrace not only the plan of the *Summa* but its implicit conclusions as well. Hence his unequivocal and unhesitating observation: "He who is ashamed to reach that far does not grasp the essence of Thomistic theology; he is ashamed of St. Thomas."[58] Father Congar, too, agrees with all this and concludes that the *Summa* offers us an inescapable option in this connection.[59]

Bearing in mind the general ideas which dominate the structure of the *Summa*, one cannot but agree with the following logical conclusion drawn by L. Ciappi:

> In the present decree relative to the Incarnation, as it is known to us from S. Scripture, Christ's predestination to be Son of God necessarily presupposes the prevision of Adam's sin. . . . For the Angelic Doctor it is not only the essence of the Incarnation and the actions of the Incarnate Word that are ordained to the redemption as to their proximate end—"ut esset nostrae salutis causa"—but the existence itself of the Icarnation is *de facto* contingent on the [divine] will to redeem the human race.[60]

2.
Blessed John Duns Scotus (d. 1308)

The contribution of Blessed John Duns Scotus to the theology of Christ's absolute primacy is as decisively important as his intervention in the controversy over Mary's Immaculate Conception.[1]

The authority of St. Bonaventure and St. Thomas in favor of an Incarnation subordinate to the Fall was such that only a man endowed with an extraordinary intellect equal to theirs could guarantee to the opposite opinion the possibility of survival. Using his theological genius, Scotus knew exactly how to give his thesis an entirely new formulation devoid of all imprecision. He presented it in its true dimension and, while he did not explicitly draw all the consequences from his own luminous principles, he did give us a glimpse of the capital importance which the doctrine of Christ's primacy has for theology in general, and for Christology in particular.

It is not through the limited perspective of "Si homo non peccasset . ." that Scotus introduces the great theme; he presents it in itself, directly. Placing himself at the heart of the mystery of Christ and of salvation, he understands the need to abandon the narrowness and ambiguities of anthropocentrism and hamartiocentrism in order to fix his attention on the very center of the salvation mystery, namely, man's free and gratuitous vocation *in Christo*—a vocation to life everlasting willed by God in His predestining goodness. The discussion of Christ's primacy no longer appears as "*a* theological question," but rather as *the* essential and all-encompassing theological datum. Obviously, in order to grasp the "novelty" and the depth of Scotus' solution it is necessary to bear in mind the fundamental principles supporting his position. These are too often neglected.

Among these basic principles we must mention especially his stress on freedom and contingency. It is here that we recognize the very heart of the

31

Scotistic vision of reality and the clue to the understanding of his whole thinking. We are not dealing with a purely philosophical conception elaborated by analyzing human experience, but an eminently theological one inasmuch as Scotus knew how to emphasize the biblical notion of God and of man in contradistinction to the anaturalistic and physicist concepts peculiar to the Greco-Aristotelians.[2]

The notion of freedom as self-determination and as a decision to do good is the general theological frame which underlines every problem having to do with the relationship between God and the world, between the supreme freedom of God and that of man. That is why Scotus regards Christian salvation as being essentially a "sacred history" and not a naturalistic metaphysics. The doctrine of Christ's primacy represents the very center and essence of the salvation mystery,[3] the very substance of the "historia salutis," and therefore that primacy will show forth in a dominant way that freedom is at the root of that history. This explains why one will never grasp the depth, originality and intrinsic motivations of Scotus' solution without an adequate knowledge of his teaching on freedom. It is precisely in freedom and love that the person expresses itself in its highest and strictest value. The "historia salutis" is simply unintelligible if we do not find in it the concrete actuation of the love-freedom factor. It is here that the profound difference between the Greek physico-naturalistic mentality and the Christian historico-personalist mentality manifests itself in a radical way. The choice must be made at this level.

1. The Argument from Predestination

In Scotus the great theme of Christ's universal primacy is closely bound up with the doctrine of His predestination. Or better still: it is proposed as the essence and the very content of divine predestination actuated in the concrete order of salvation in such a manner that Christ's predestination substantially coincides with His primacy.

Having treated of predestination in reference to the glory of Christ and to the hypostatic union, Scotus introduces the problem thus: "Sed hic sunt duo dubia. Primum utrum praedestinatio ista (i.e., Christi) praeexigat necessario lapsum naturae humanae; quod videntur sonare multae auctoritates."[4]

This formulation of the question is, of course, absolutely new. The Doctor thus situates the problem in its authentic roots, in its exact physiognomy, in its vast theological dimension. By relating the subject to predestination we can understand better the mission of Christ in the plan of salvation and hence His role in reference to all divine works *ad extra*. It also means referring the entire natural and supernatural orders to the free and most wise will of God, to His supremely gratuitous love as to the ultimate principle that rules, illumines, and dominates everything.

In its most general and fundamental meaning, the idea of predestination tells us in the first place that in carrying out the plan of salvation, God's will is in no way conditioned by creatures but is essentially sovereign and free. God's freedom (i.e., His love) is the beginning of all things; it is the ultimate explanation of the order of salvation which embraces both nature and grace.

Scotus defines predestination as follows: 'Praedestinatio est praeordinatio alicujus ad gloriam principaliter et ad alia in ordine ad gloriam.'[5] Predestination is, then, directly, an ordination to eternal glory as to an end. Besides, in an indirect way it implies also the modalities, the means, the concrete and necessary realities required to obtain the end.

In this there is agreement between Scotus and St. Thomas,[6] although they differ in the manner they relate predestination to the will of God. Both teach that the end and the specific and total terminus of predestination is the glory to be attained, while grace, merit and the will's cooperation are the means to the end. The means depend upon, and are subordinated to, the end. For Scotus, as for St. Thomas, predestination is *ante praevisa merita*, that is to say, absolutely gratuitous; it is the gift of God's free, creative love; it is an act of pure benevolence, a sublime gift of God who wishes to share His own life with His creatures.

Now—Scotus proceeds—if predestination is a gratuitous gift of God which in no way depends on the creature, we will have to say, *a fortiori*, that it precedes the prevision of sin which is a defect and a privation. It cannot be conditioned by anything positive—and much less negative—on the part of creatures. The Subtle Doctor points out that if the predestination of all (men and angels) takes place absolutely "before" the prevision of sin and hence independently of it, we must say the same in the case of Christ who is the greatest of the predestined. In Him the general notion of predestination becomes a reality in the most perfect manner: "Multo magis [hoc] est verum de praedestinatione illius animae quae praedestinabatur ad summam gloriam."[7] We repeat: Christ's predestination can in no way depend on the prevision of sin. It is the result of the most exceptional love of God freely and gratuitously wishing to communicate Himself and to share His own divine life with the God-Man in the most perfect way.

At this juncture, Scotus' reasoning brings to light the causal and ontological relationship of Christ's predestination to all other predestinations in order to show even more forcefully its independence from Adam's sin.

This is the famous argument based on the "ordinate volens'—the very pivot of Scotus' demonstration:

> Universaliter, enim, ordinate volens prius videtur velle hoc quod est fini propinquius, et ita sicut prius vult gloriam alicui quam gratiam, ita etiam inter praedestinatos, quibus vult gloriam, ordinate prius videtur velle gloriam illi, quem vult esse proximum fini, et ita huic animae prius vult gloriam quam alicui alteri animae velit gloriam, et prius cuilibet alteri gloriam et gratiam quam praevideat illi opposita istorum habituum.[8]

In order to assess adequately the theological value of the above reasoning it is necessary to recall that, according to Scotus, the will—and in a very special way the divine will—is eminently rational. It is not only a self-determination, but a self-determining toward a foreknown good. The will is not an indeterminate, indifferent potency, but a conscious self-determination toward good. That is why the more perfect the knowledge (which, however, is never the *cause* of the free act!) the more perfect also the will-freedom.[9] The "ordinate volens," applied to God, indicates precisely a will that expresses and lives in itself the maximum of intellectuality and of holiness: "Sicut universaliter libertas stat cum apprehensione praevia, ita summa libertas stat cum summa apprehensione praevia."[10]

Again: Scotus, too, accepts the validity of the well known principle *Ens et bonum convertuntur*. The good is a transcendental property of being. For this reason the adequate and proper object of the divine will-freedom is only the infinite being of God who is precisely the greatest good. The perfection of God's will, therefore, has two aspects: a) as an activity of the divine nature; and b) as a free relation to the greatest good which is the divine nature itself. The former is an ontological perfection of the divine will, while the latter is a moral perfection. According to W. Hoeres,

> Scotus distinguishes these two aspects with extraordinary clarity. The first, the ontological perfection, belongs to the will when considered in itself. The second, inasmuch as the will has reference to the object. The two are mutually dependent in the closest way, since the exact content of the will's essence is precisely its ordination to the rational.[11]

Bearing in mind these two aspects of the divine will as an essentially perfect and holy freedom, it follows that we cannot possibly affirm, without denying such perfection in God, that He ordains that which is more perfect to that which is less perfect. Indeed, as being is to being, so is the good to the good. The ontological gradation of beings expresses, then, in its reference, a hierarchy of being-good which is a manifestation of the "ordinate volens" and cannot be subverted without denying that God is, in fact, "ordinatissime volens." Thus it would be a denial of the rationality and morality of the divine will to affirm, for instance, that man has been made for the dog, or in order to rear or breed dogs, in such a way that the good of the dogs conditions the *existence* of man and exhausts its finality.

To state that Christ's existence was occasioned by Adam's sin and that the primary reason for His coming was to be a remedy for that sin means exactly the overturning of the scale of values "being-good." It means declaring that the most exalted creature, the God-Man, is occasioned by sin and subordinated to man. All this involves the denial of the "ordinate volens" and of the moral perfection of the divine will. Turning around this untenable solution, we will have to say, on the contrary, in virtue of the axiom "ordinate volens," that God willed Christ not only independently of sin and without essential reference to it, but that He willed angels and men—indeed all creatures—for the sake of Christ because He is the "fini propinquior." In other words, God willed Christ as the archetype, the cause, the end, the mediator of all the predestined. And since every predestination by nature "precedes" the prevision of the Fall and is independent of it, *a fortiori* the predestination of Christ cannot depend on it either.

Furthermore, since the natural order is *de facto* willed by God for the supernatural order which has its beginning and end in Christ Jesus, it follows, in virtue of the same axiom "ordinate volens," that the entire universe is willed by God for the sake of Christ, and not the other way around.

In his often difficult Latin, Scotus describes predestination as a gratuitous act by which God freely communicates Himself *ad extra* but with due gradation and observing a hierarchy among the various creatures, with the God-Man as their center. In Christ God willed to communicate Himself in a manner so sublime as to introduce all creatures into the very bosom of the Blessed Trinity. Christ, as the "summum opus Dei," is therefore the first in the mind of God. He is the archetype and the paradigm of every other communication in the order both of grace and of nature. Describing the "historia salutis" and the intermingling of causalities in the economy actually willed by God, the Subtle Doctor writes in an equally famous text:

> God first loves Himself; secondly, He loves Himself for others, and this is an ordered love; thirdly, He wishes to be loved by the One who can love Him in the highest way—speaking of the love of someone who is extrinsic to Him; and fourthly, He foresees the union of that nature which must love Him with the greatest love even if no one had

fallen.[12]

2. Love is at the Root of it All

In the text of Scotus cited immediately above, we see a perfect framing and delineation of the doctrine of predestination with everything it implies in reference to Christ and to the other creatures, leaving aside those arguments which have only the appearance of "proofs". These arguments either presuppose the primacy as already demonstrated, or else are practically worthless.

In the first place, the source and cause of predestination is *the love of God*. No need to recall again that, for Scotus, love is synonymous with freedom and will: A free act and an act of love are one and the same thing. The root of the exact relationship between God and creatures is only the divine love-freedom. The essential contingency of creatures finds its *raison d'être* in the free love of God. No theologian has ever succeeded in delineating this basic God-creature relationship the way Scotus has.[13] *A fortiori*, the root of the supernatural order must be sought exclusively in God's gratuitous love, in His creative goodness.

For this very reason, the most sublime product of God's love *ad extra* is necessarily a lofty Lover, one who is capable of loving God in a perfect manner. Corresponding to God's creative love (the ultimate and dominating reason of His *ad extra* communication) we have Christ Jesus (the most perfect of all works *ad extra*) embodying the supreme response to God's love. Love is, therefore, the greatest and fundamental "value" both of God's activity and of the rational creature. Love, which is rational freedom, is thus the supreme expression of the relationship between God the Father and Christ. Love is not a relationship between two "things," between two "objects," between two "beings," but between two *persons*. It is a love-freedom that designates a person as such in its precise mode of existing and operating. As a consequence, for Scotus, all the actions of Christ must be theologically understood as so many answers of His love to that of the Father.

It is now evident and beyond discussion that the reasoning used by the Subtle Doctor radically transforms the arguments previously advanced to prove Christ's independence from the Fall. We have in mind especially the arguments based on the Neoplatonic axiom, *Bonum est diffusivum sui*, and those which conceived Christ as the perfection and crown of the universe. As noted before, Alexander of Hales attributed great weight to them.

But Scotus vigorously rejects the idea that Christ was the product of a "demand" arising from the *Bonum diffusivum sui*. There is nothing more contrary to his thought than this *necessary* action predicated of God. This impersonal, physico-naturalistic emanationism peculiar to Platonism is totally repugnant to our Doctor and diametrically at odds with his theology. According to him, all operations are divided into two essential modalities. The "agere naturaliter," common to all infra-personal realities, is an acting due to a motion received *ab extrinseco*; even the intellect operates "naturaliter." But the second mode of operation, the *agere libere*, is proper only to the will. We have here a motion by way of self-determination, *ab intrinseco*. And it is this that constitutes the genuine worth of the person. Scotus unceasingly declares that the only reason for the existence of creatures is the divine freedom; that freedom is a mode of acting radically different from the "agere naturaliter." This explains why Scotus rejects the well-known argumentation based on the *Bonum diffusivum sui* understood in the Neoplatonic sense, as a necessary exigency of communication.[14]

Unlike St. Bonaventure and Alexander of Hales, our Doctor does not even hint at any *a priori* deductions from the divine nature. As to the argument based on Christ's being the "perfection" of the universe—an argument so frequently and erroneously attributed to Scotus—[15] it is clear that he affirms the very opposite. Indeed, in virtue of the axiom that the less perfect is always for the sake of the more perfect and that God is "ordinatissime volens," we must say that the universe and man were willed for the sake of Christ, and not the other way around. Christ is not the "crown" and the "zenith" of the universe, but rather its root, its end, its *raison d'être*; and this—note well—not because of any aprioristic exigency on the part of the world, but exclusively because God freely and gratuitously willed all things to have their center and foundation *in Christo Jesu*. In fact, not even the intrinsic perfection of Christ Himself nor the glory which He renders to the Father should be regarded as the *primary* reason for the Incarnation. The existence of Christ and all the benefits which accrue to man and to the universe owing to that existence, flow primarily from God's free love. They are diffused to all creatures by Christ and in Christ as the *primum volitum*. This is the profound sense of Scotus' lapidary assertions in that celebrated text cited earlier, which expresses the order of the *ordinate volens*:

> God first loves Himself; secondly, He loves Himself for others, and this is an ordered love; thirdly, He wishes to be loved by One who can love Him in the highest way—speaking of the love of someone extrinsic to Him; and fourthly, He foresees the union of that nature which must love Him with the greatest love. . . .

Salvation history is thus removed from all naturalism and necessitarianism and is perceived in its essential values. In this way Scotus not only situates himself at the correct point of departure—salvation history—in order to outline the doctrine of Christ's primacy, but he also sets down the basic theologico-biblical principles to understand it. He breaks out of a narrow horizon; he refutes flimsy arguments; he discloses the true panorama of a consistent Christology. The notion of predestination, with everything it implies concerning divine freedom and order, furnishes him the right clue to unravel the mystery.

It is of interest to note here that the two modern theologians who have treated the theme of Christ's primacy in depth and with the greatest care— M. J. Scheeben and K. Barth—bring out the decisive value of Scotus' perspective. Although approaching the question from a different angle, they present it with a similar amplitude of vision and correctly regard Christ's absolute primacy as the very heart and essence of Christian theology and Revelation.

3. Consequences

Christ's predestination, then, with everything it implies, is at the center of salvation history; it is the beginning and the end of all the works of God. By God's free will, all the orders of creatures, every gift and reality, hinge on Christ; creation, grace, glory, faith and theology are all "christological." Christ's primacy is inscribed in the very ontological density and in the salvific value which God achieves in all created realities. All this is so, not owing to an exigency on the part of man or the universe, not even because it is somehow required by God's essential attributes, but solely and exclusively because God has freeely chosen this order of things. It is not, therefore, a question of inquiring into what God could have done, but of grasping the fundamental lines of the plan which He actually selected and carried out.[16]

It follows *a fortiori* that the Incarnation cannot be determined by Adam's sin; the very notion of predestination excludes it, as indeed it is excluded by the rationality and morality of the *ordinatissime volens* who is God. To these propositions, Scotus adds other arguments which flow as corollaries. For example, it is impossible to hold that the Incarnation is a *bonum occasionatum*—a good occasioned by sin or by man—while the glory of all the other elect (angels and men) is never occasioned but directly willed by God "before" the prevision of other events and of all those factors which are but means to the end. Again: It is unlikely, indeed untenable, that before his sin Adam was predestined to a glory that was much lesser than the one to which he was predestined after his disobedience. In effect, first he would have been predestined to glory without Christ, while after his sin (and because of it) he would have been predestined to glory in Christ—the latter being intrinsically more perfect than the former. Finally, Scotus notes, if Christ had been predestined only as a redeemer, He would have rejoiced over Adam's prevarication, since He would have owed His existence to it. Now, no one is ever predestined "tantum quia alius praevisus est casurus." Only Christ, the greatest of the predestined, would find Himself in this unique—and humiliating—situation of owing His predestination to God, yes, but also to Adam's sinful act as a prerequisite![17]

4. Those Troublesome "Instantia Rationis"

Some theologians claim that Scotus' exposition implies a certain anthropomorphism in God inasmuch as he places several "befores" and "afters" in the one, most simple act of divine will. Indeed, the plan of the *ordinate volens* affirms that God "first" loves Himself; then "secondly" He loves Himself for the benefit of others; "then" He wills Christ, etc. All this seems to be repugnant to the simplicity of God. This is why L. Molina, S.J. (d. 1601) solemnly intoned: "Exterminanda videntur instantia Scoti. . . ."[18] And to think that Molina, the theologian of the "scientia media," is an inimitable virtuoso when it comes to finding antecedent, intermediate, and subsequent *signa rationis* in God! Not a few Thomists, in their effort to escape the very "troublesome" argument based on the *ordinate volens*, adopt Molina's viewpoint in this connection. Thus L. Ciappi, O.P. writes:

> Let us, then, allow that a man "ordinate volens" wills first the end and then the means ordained to the end. As for ourselves, let us be satisfied knowing, with Aquinas, that in the divine will and intelligence there is not priority of time or of volition or of causality, but everything is simultaneous.[19]

But we ask: Has any theologian ever denied God's absolute simplicity? Surely not Scotus; nor, for that matter, any of his disciples. And, incidentally, do not the Thomists and the Molinists make use of the *signa rationis* to the point of exasperation in the controversy over predestination and grace? In the tracts *De Deo Uno, De Deo Trino,* and *De Gratia,* the recourse to *signa rationis* is universally accepted as necessary by those who wish to speak intelligently about God. To insist on excluding them only when discussing the Incarnation leaves the impression that these theologians are anxious to evade the force of the Scotistic argument. As a matter of fact, when the

Thomists affirm, as they always do, that Christ's predestination *pre*supposes in God the *pre*vision of sin, are they not actually, though implictly, postulating *signa rationis* in God?

The need to distinguish a "before" and an "after" in the divine decree is due to the fact that every reality is an order whose various parts or elements have certain relationships that bind them together. According to whether we are dealing with the logical or the ontological order, we will have a logical or a causal-ontological priority, and the two priorities do not always coincide. Since every finite "order" depends on God, "necesse est," writes St. Thomas, "quod ratio ordinis rerum in finem in mente divina praeexistat."[20]

In our thought-process we humans are bound by categories of time and space, and that is why we often use these categories in reference to certain notions which actually transcend time and space. Thus we say that the cause is "before" the effect, even if this does not *per se* imply temporality. The "before" helps us to designate the manner of relationship between two extremes. Again, when we say that God is "before" the world, we are employing a chronological expression to describe a qualitative relation of cause to effect, even though we realize only too well that in God there is no time. Hence, when we distinguish a "before" and "after" in the divine will or intellect we do not mean to anthropomorphize God in any way; we merely wish to express the cause-effect relationship which exists among things inasmuch as they have their origin in God.

Furthermore, we must make a distinction between the logical and the ontological orders. This is indispensable if we wish to reach an accurate evaluation of Scotus' solution relative to the primacy of Christ, and if we must overcome the many difficulties that are raised against it. The logical order concerns the ambit of pure possibilities. In such an order of things, the perfect is "before" the less than perfect, the simple "before" the composite, and so on. Logical priority is not temporal but only rational.

In the ontological order, however, the cause is "before" the effect, the greater being "before" the lesser being. Ontological priority, although expressed with a terminology borrowed from the space-time ambit, is not reducible to time or space. For example, we say that Abraham is "before" Isaac inasmuch as the former is the latter's father. Now, this relationship exists also in God, eternally: God wills eternally—not temporally—Abraham as the cause of Isaac; which is why we say that God wills one "before" the other, without thereby introducing any chronology in God.

In connection with the *signa rationis*, St. Francis de Sales (d. 1622) makes the following limpid observation:

Now when saying, Theotimus, that God had seen and willed first one thing and then secondly another . . . , I meant this in the sense I declared before, namely, that though all this took place in a most singular and simple act, yet in that act the order, distinction and dependence of things were no less observed than if there had been indeed several acts in the understanding and will of God. And since every well-ordered will which determines itself to love several objects equally present, loves better and above all the rest that which is most lovable; it follows that the sovereign Providence, making his eternal purpose and design of all that he would produce, first willed and preferred by excellence the most amiable object of his love which is Our Saviour; and then other creatures in order, according as they more or less belong to the service, honour and glory of him.[21]

Another premise not to be forgotten if we wish to understand Scotus' thought is the well-known distinction between the "ordo intentionis" and the "ordo executionis." Both concern the concrete order of salvation willed by God, but from different angles. Contrary to what some seem to think, the "ordo intentionis" does not refer to the orbit of pure possibilities and the "ordo executionis" to that of reality; both are moments of the same concrete order.

Following the example of St. Paul (Eph. 1:3ff), we can see the divine plan of salvation as a design that God has within Himself and which He wishes to carry out gradually and in an orderly way in time. It is only at the end, in the *eschaton*, that the "ordo executionis" completely fulfills the "ordo intentionis." The knowledge of the intentional order is extremely important if we wish to assess properly the order of execution; the latter's outline, its meaning, and the various factors that integrate it can be grasped with precision only by considering the whole which governs them. Being a free act of God, the "ordo intentionis" of the salvation plan cannot be deduced from the notion of God, of man, or of the universe. We can get a glimpse of it only through Revelation and from its fulfillment in the order of execution.

It is in Christ Jesus that sacred history has reached its end, although not all its effects have been displayed. The *eschaton*, which is the point of contact of the two orders, allows us to understand the "ordo intentionis" in the best way. It is the terminal point of sacred history that will unfold the criterion and the measure to evaluate each aspect of the history itself; it will be a clue to obtain an exact "reading" for each component part.

Now, according to Revelation, this *eschaton* consists in the creatures' sharing of eternal life *as members of the Body of Christ*; it consists in being introduced, as "filii in Filio," to the *koinonia* of the divine Persons. This is the plan of salvation in its ultimate realization. Therefore, it is precisely by taking Christ as the point of departure, as the center and total principle of salvation, that we can perceive the outline of the divine plan and become aware of the relationship that everything has to Christ. Since Christ is *primus in ordine essendi* in the plan of salvation, He must be likewise *primus in ordine cognoscendi*. He is, in other words, the supreme principle of intelligibility of all things—of the universe, of men, of grace, of glory. That means that in the concrete order freely chosen by God, a theology that tries to explain created realities and the supernatural while prescinding from Christ, is attempting the impossible.

Obviously, we have been dealing here with notions that are widely accepted in theology. Nevertheless, we deemed it necessary to recall them because Scotus' thought is too frequently misunderstood owing precisely to the fact that these distinctions are not always kept in mind.

5. The "Ordo Amoris"

The most fundamental consequences deriving from the formulation and solution which Scotus gives to the problem of Christ's primacy may be seen especially in connection with the capital questions of (a) the unity of the salvific plan, and (b) the relationship between goodness and justice. By stressing the unity and the irreversibility of the divine plan of salvation, Scotus eliminates the dualism already noted in the solutions suggested by St. Bonaventure and St. Thomas. There are not two orders of salvation—one before sin, which abstracted from Christ, and the other after sin, which hinges on Him. Jesus did not *become* the Head of a universe that pre-existed Him and which had already been ordained to a supernatural end. He is definitely not an "afterthought"; He presides over the very origin of all things in the mind of God. The breach created by the Fall was not decisive in the sense that it brought about a change in the divine design; it was not a total fracture; the initial supernatural orientation to Christ remains firm and intact. According to the predestining will of God and from the very beginning of God's works, Christ is the solid and unshakable foundation of our "adoption in Christ," as the Latin Fathers phrase it, or of man's "divinization in Christ," as the Greek Fathers prefer to call it. No creature or action of a creature can possibly render the divine plan inefficacious, mutable, reversible. *God is faithful,* as Sacred Scripture constantly teaches, precisely in order to underline the infallible execution of His plan. Actually, it is inconceivable for an economy that has already been decided upon and has been assigned an end, to be replaced by another having a different end, without involving a metaphysical breach between the former and the latter.

Jesus cannot "become" a new end without a new creation being involved—unless we wish to tamper with the universally accepted meaning of the word "end."

It follows from this that Jesus Christ is not only the center of the creature's *reditus in Deum*, as St. Bonaventure and St. Thomas taught, but also the beginning of our *exitus a Deo*. He is not only the one who leads us back to God, but also the one in whom we egress from God. Our return to God *in Christo*, taken at its true value, necessarily postulates our egress from God *in Christo*. Sacred Scripture, especially St. Paul, clearly teaches that all God's works *ad extra* are dominated by Christ in every moment and in every sense (cf. Col. 1:15-19). The *eschaton* undoubtedly discloses to us the final moment; hence, creation, the initial moment, cannot be a neutral, a-theological premise; grace cannot be a-Christic first and Christic later. Briefly: In God's mind, from the very beginning, everything is Christological and Christocentric.

This overcoming of an illogical theory which tends to brush Christ to the margin, and to replace the biblical notion of Christ's absolute centrality with a metaphysics of creation and grace, is one of the richest and most important conquests of Scotus' theology, and—why not say it?—of theology as a whole. The Incarnation presupposes, not the Fall but the free will of God. The basic effect of the Incarnation, as far as men are concerned is their supernatural election, adoption, and divinization *in Christo Jesu*. It is not the reparation of a sinful act, but the total orientation of the entire human race to Christ. It is not the surmounting of a deficiency of the moral order, but the divine surmounting of man's "metaphysical deficiency," so that from being a pure creature he becomes an adopted child of God *in Christo Jesu*, a sharer in the very life of God. And it is precisely from these two different perspectives (i.e., the overcoming of the creatures' moral deficiency as against the overcoming of their metaphysical deficiency) that we can grasp the profound difference of the two viewpoints under discussion.

The present and concrete economy of salvation in Christ Jesus, then, is essentially and primarily an *ordo amoris*, by which we mean simply the free, gratuitous and unconditioned communication of divine life *in Christo Jesu*.

Within the framework of this *ordo amoris* we can see how obsolete has become the question of the so-called "motive" of the Incarnation (understood as the cause moving the divine will) and especially its hypothetical formulation. The "mover" or "motive" of a free action is intrinsic to freedom itself. According to Scotus, freedom is not mere indetermination, not even mere self-determination; this would be nothing but indifference or irrational spontaneity and hence impossible in the person as such. For the Subtle Doctor, freedom means self-determination toward that which is good, an autonomous decision for the good. It is, therefore, acting in a highly moral manner. Thus we can say that the notion-reality of the good is essential to the constitution of freedom. Nor should we forget that the will, according to Scotus, is never determined to act *ab extrinseco*. In other words, it is not moved; it moves itself by way of a self-decision without which it would cease to be a "will-freedom."

The will's relation to the good may be conceived from a twofold viewpoint. First, the will may be related to a good distinct from itself, external to itself, and hence a good to be obtained. Under this aspect, the good is the *terminus* of the will, not the cause of the volition. Secondly, the good may be considered as a good willed for its own sake inasmuch as it is a good or the greatest good. Not even in this case is the good a "motive" of the will, but the terminus and the *reason* of its volition. Especially in the case of God's will we cannot think of good external to it and determining it to action. As far as God is concerned, absolutley nothing can be a good to be obtained, for the cogent reason that He is the *bonum per essentiam*.

We cannot, therefore, speak of anything as being the "motive" of the Incarnation. There is only a *reason* for it—the wisest reason guiding the divine will *ad extra*. The *ordo amoris* is the only reason for the Incarnation. And it is the *ordo amoris* that now leads us to consider another very important aspect of the Scotistic solution to the question of Christ's primacy, namely, the relationship existing between the Incarnation and the redemption.

6. The Redemption Within the Incarnational Framework

From everything we have seen, it emerges clearly that Scotus regards the redemption as being one aspect of the Incarnation. Hence, contrary to the view of St. Bonaventure and St. Thomas, the Incarnation is not for the sake of the redemption, but *vice versa*.

The adoption-divinization in Christ, which signifies essentially the surmounting of man's metaphysical deficiency, does not postulate sin as a point of departure, but only man's fallible limitation. Freeing us from sin, therefore, is a successive moment, one case to which the divinizing function of the Incarnation is applied. In reference to man, the redemption is the execution of a potency of the Incarnation due to the fact that man, because of his sin, is not only in a state of fallible limitation but also in a state of actuated fallibility. But this does not change the meaning of the fundamental dimension of the Incarnation. As far as Christ Himself is concerned, death has the sense of a "crossing over" to resurrection; it is the Incarnation in its process of becoming, in its historical development in order to reach the *eschaton*, its perfection; it is the actuation of the Incarnation as history. This leads Scotus to a radical critique and overturning of St. Anselm's hamartiocentirc theory which so decisively influenced the theology of subsequent centuries. As he approaches the theme of redemption, the Subtle Doctor begins by faithfully presenting the Anselmian theology of the *Cur Deus Homo* which he condenses in the following four conclusions:

> Primo, videndum est, secundum Anselmum, quod necessarium fuit hominem redimi. Secundo, quod non potuit redimi sine satisfactione. Tertio, quod facienda erat satisfactio a Deo-Homine. Quarto, quod convenientior modus fuit hic, scilicet per passionem Christi.[22]

In all of the above conclusions Scotus rejects the character of necessity. As in the Incarnation, so also in the redemption, the governing principle is always the divine *ordo amoris*; hence, no necessity, but only gratuitousness and freedom.

> Omnia hujusmodi quae facta sunt a Christo circa redemptionem nostram, non fuerunt necessaria, nisi praesupposita ordinatione divina quae sic ordinavit fieri, et tunc tantum necessitate consequentiae necessarium fuit Christum pati; sed tamen, totum fuit contingens simpliciter, et antecedens et consequens.[23]

In the plan of salvation, then, according to Scotus, one can in no way speak of necessity, much less of a necessity imposed by man's fault. The existence of Christ, His life and His death are the effect of God's free design based on love. They are not dictated by the ''logic'' of sin and satisfaction. Any and every form of necessitarianism is excluded by Scotus in its very root. The will, especially the divine will, always moves itself; it is never moved *ab extrinseco*.

This explains why there is no contest or tension between the *ordo amoris* and the *ordo justitiae*, since the latter is but a facet of the former. There is no justice that necessarily demands a satisfaction through the death of the God-Man. All the concrete modalities of the Incarnation, including the Passion and death on the Cross, are but different manifestations of the *ordo amoris*. This, as Scotus points out, stimulates our filial admiration and gratitude toward God:

> Ex quo enim aliter potuisset homo redimi et tamen ex sua libera voluntate Deus sic redimit, multum ei tenemur et amplius quam si sic necessario et non aliter potuissemus fuisse redempti.[24]

How are we to judge St. Anselm's hamartiocentrism and all that flows from it?

> Si volumus salvare Anselmum, dicamus quod omnes rationes suae procedunt praesupposita ordinatione divina quae sic ordinavit hominem redimi; . . . nulla tamen necessitas fuit.[25]

In other words, in order to "save" St. Anselm, we have to abandon his hamartiocentrism with its consequent necessitarianism and replace it with the *ordo amoris* which is the *ratio* of everything. But then, what remains of *Cur Deus Homo*? At any rate, Scotus rejects the Anselmian thesis because it is incompatible with the absolute primacy of Jesus Christ and the biblical concept of freedom.

7. The "Passibility" of the Incarnation

The explanation given by Scotus of Christ's primacy is limpid and profound. The theme is carried back to its real roots and is formulated in its right dimension. In the present, concrete economy of salvation Jesus Christ is the First Predestined and for that very reason the exemplary, efficient and final cause of the election and predestination of all others. Jesus Christ, then, is not for the sake of creatures; it is the other way around.

An objection constantly raised against Scotus was to the effect that his solution ran counter to the "auctoritates" of Sacred Scripture and the Fathers. St. Bonaventure and St. Thomas were so convinced that God had become man "propter nos homines et propter nostram salutem," that they rejected any other reasoning to the contrary.

In Scotus' thinking, however, these "auctoritates" undoubtedly witness to a revealed fact, but it is not legitimate to make an affirmative proposition into an éxclusive one. To do so would be a paralogism leading to absurd conclusions. To state that God became man in order to redeem us is one thing; to state that He became man *only* to redeem us is another thing.

> Omnes autem auctoritates possunt exponi sic, scilicet quod Christus non venisset ut redemptor, nisi homo cecidisset, nec forte ut passibilis.[26]

The Subtle Doctor recalls here the distinction (already known to Bonaventure and Aquinas) between the substance of the Incarnation and its modality. The substance was supposed to have been predestined before all creatures, and *a fortiori* before the Fall, while the modality was willed after the prevision of sin. In Scotus' answer, which was adopted by virtually all his disciples, let us note some affirmations. In the first place: "Christus non venisset ut redemptor nisi homo cecidisset," and again: "Nec redemptor fuisset nisi homo pecasset."

From the above it is evident that, for Scotus, "to redeem" and "to free from sin" are the same thing. In this he is in perfect agreement with the theological mentality of his time. With such a premise, the conclusion follows logically, namely, the passible mode of the Incarnation must have been willed by God "after the prevision of Adam's sin. More: Christ's Passion and death, at least *de facto*, are willed on account of sin, and so the primary meaning of Christ's death is expiatory and satisfactory. On this particular point, Scotus adheres to the Anselmian tradition. There is, however, a second element on which Scotus differs from that tradition: Christ's Passion and death are connected with the reparation of sin by God's *free* will; they are not necessitated by a condign satisfaction for sin, as Anselm thought. That is why Scotus says: "Christus non venisset ut redemptor, nisi homo cecidisset, *nec forte ut passibilis.*"

In other words, the passibility is not demanded by the Incarnation; the latter is possible without the former. But not even sin necessarily postualtes the passibility. In fact, even abstracting from sin, possibility is not *per se* incompatible with the Incarnation. Scotus clearly states that even if there had been no sin from which to be redeemed, the Incarnation *perhaps* would have been "impassible," though not necessarily so.

In this way Scotus again opposes any form of Anselmian necessitarianism. Even if Christ were impassible, a condign reparation for sin would be possible by means of an act of love toward His Father. Not only the Incarnation, but also its passibility and the death on the Cross are absolutely gratuitous: "Omnia quae sunt facta a Christo circa redemptionem nostram, non fuerunt necessaria nisi praesupposita ordinatione divina." Christ's passibility and His death on the Cross were willed by God in order to draw us all the more forcefully to His love: "Ad alliciendum nos ad amorem suum, ut credo, hoc praecipue fuit, et quia voluit hominem amplius teneri Deo."[27] Note how the great theme of the *ordo amoris* is always present as the *ultima ratio* of everything without exception.[28]

8. Scotus' Incongruities

At this juncture we should like to make some observations on the way Scotus' thought runs into some incongruities with his previously embraced principles relative to the primacy of Christ. The matter is aggravated by the fact that most of his followers are guilty of the same incongruities. It is true enough that the clear biblical teaching concerning the absolute primacy of Christ compels us to understand the statements on the redemption in a much wider context, as Scotus does. However, the traditional distinction between the substance and the passible modality of the Incarnation, with all its implications, does not seem to harmonize with the primacy of Christ. Does not that distinction make the greatest work of Christ (His death on the Cross) depend on man's sin? If so, are we not actually letting in through the window, as it were, the very thing we chased out through the door? Briefly: Is not Scotus somehow subordinating Christ to sin—not in His existence, to be sure—but in the climactic action of His life, His death on the Cross?

It is true that the Subtle Doctor, unlike so many of his followers, vigorously underlines the gratuitous divine disposition regarding the death of the Savior. For him, this death is not required as a necessary condition for man's redemption from sin, but only as a modality which expresses in a marvelous fashion the love of God and of Christ. The nexus between passibility and sin is thus reduced to a minimum; sin appears, then, as a mere "conditio sine qua non," and not the *cause* of the passibility and of the resulting death. Nevertheless, the nexus remains and hence also a shadow over the doctrine of the primacy.

The Thomists have always, and rightly, raised a very grave objection against the distinction between the substance and the modality of the Incarnation. With one single act God willed the Incarnation to take place in a concrete and determinate manner, in its substance *and* in its modality. One cannot say that God first willed the substance in an indetermined manner, and later in a concrete manner after the prevision of man's sin; the first indetermined volition is neither intelligible, nor, therefore feasible. Or else one would have to suppose that God first willed Christ to be impassible (substance and modality), and then after the prevision of sin, changed the modality, making it passible. But this is obviously absurd, and it would be equivalent to admitting a determination "from below" which reflects on Christ. Isn't that precisely the very thing Scotus wishes to avoid at all costs?

The Thomists conclude, correctly, that predestination concerns both the substance and the modality with one single efficacious act. Hence, if Christ is willed "before" the prevision of sin, He is willed as Redeemer. But from this premise (which is correct), they argue (wrongly): since the redemption presupposes sin requiring redemption, it is necessary to affirm that Christ was willed "after" the prevision of sin and because of it. But this deduction compromises the most certain doctrine of Christ's absolute primacy, which is why Scotus vigorously rejects it, as we have seen.

There must be some obscure, erroneous point which creates the apparent insurmountability of the two positions, and which in Scotus' position itself gives rise to incongruities and inconsistencies. And it seems to us that the troublesome obscurity in question is due to an inadequate understanding of the term "redemption."

In the Scholastic period, "to redeem" was the exclusive equivalent of "to free from sin." Subsequent controversies with Protestants shapened even more this persuasion within the two respective Schools, and this gave rise to insoluble oppositions.

Scotus, with an intuition of pure genius, had succeeded in solving the difficulty concerning Mary's Immaculate Conception (a difficulty created by the notion of Christ's universal redemption) by introducing the concept of "perfect (preservative) redemption." Now, in the doctrine of Christ's primacy, it is again the notion of redemption that creates the fundamental obstacle. Here, too, in his elaboration of the doctrine of the primacy, Scotus had the happy geniality of conceiving the relationship between Christ and men in its ontological dimension rather than in its moral dimension. That is to say, the primary and fundamental meaning of the Incarnation is the election, the adoption and divinization of men in Christ Jesus, and not the reparation of a broken friendship; it is the surmounting of the creature's metaphysical deficiency much more than the surmounting of a deficiency of the moral order.

The Subtle Doctor, then, had set down the basic principles that should have freed us from a too-narrow notion of redemption. Unfortunately, he did not reach a clear and explicit formulation along these lines, as he had done for the Immaculate Conception. And this shadow, lengthened by his followers, was cast for centuries to come, over his elucidation of Christ's universal primacy.

9. A Summary Evaluation

Even a schematic exposition of Scotus' thought has at once allowed us a glimpse at the profound originality of his theology concerning the primacy of Christ. In this field he is a true pioneer. Taking as a point of departure the idea of predestination in its full biblical sense, Scotus identifies it radically with the predestination of Christ. Every predestination is nothing but a sharing in that of Christ. Hence, the primacy no longer appears as a marginal thesis, but becomes the very heart of theology for the good reason that Christ is the center, the principle, the beginning and end of the divine plan of salvation and hence of all God's works *ad extra*.[29]

The fundamental consequence of this manner of envisaging Christ's primacy is the priority and absolute preponderance of the *ordo amoris* over the *ordo justitiae*. Every hamartiocentrism and every anthropocentrism is thus thoroughly eradicated. The center, the soul of Christ's life and activities is His love toward the Father. The notions of expiation, satisfaction, sacrificial death, and reparation must all be understood within the absolutely pre-eminent frame of Christ's love as an answer to that of the Father.

Strictly speaking, therefore, there can be no question of the Incarnation having a "motive" or a "cause"; it has only a *reason*. In effect, God's love is creative. He does not love that which He finds lovable, as is the case with creatures, but He produces that which He loves, since God does not depend on anything.[30] Saying that there is a *reason* for the Incarnation we mean that the mystery has an explanation, an internal intelligiblity. The explanation consists in being a supreme communication of God's free and all-powerful love.

A third affirmation results from the above. There is among creatures a hierarchy which is based on their degree of being (natural and supernatural), a hierarchy that is the sequel of their predestination by God and of His creative love. In virtue of this hierarchy, Sacred Scripture tells us that man, as the image of God, is the king and center of creation. Now, as the universe is a reflection of man, so all creatures are a reflection of Christ. He is their archetype, their "firstborn," their *raison d'être*, their final end. It is from Him that they receive their ultimate meaning.

Since Scotus has included the redemption within the frame of the Incarnation and has described salvation as the surmounting of the ontological deficiency of the person and of the creature's freedom more than the surmounting of a moral deficiency (i.e. that of sin), some have accused him of having underestimated the redemption.[31] They say that while St. Francis of Assisi always experienced a most ardent love for Christ's Passion, his followers, the Franciscans, are oriented in the opposite direction.[32]

The accusation does not hold up. Scotus, in fact, makes it possible for us to grasp the profound reason for St. Francis' devotion to the Passion. The *ordo amoris* which dominates the theology of the Subtle Doctor throws a brilliant light on the most essential aspect of the Savior's sufferings and death. St. Francis' soul, being eminently evangelical, was aroused, not by the juridical outlook of the *ordo justitiae*, but by the irresistible appeal of the *ordo amoris*.

The above concluding observations are not meant to convey the idea that Scotus elaborated a perfect and definitive theology of Christ's primacy. The history of theology shows that he did not. There are in his solution a few infelicitous points that seem incompatible with the basic principles he himself set down. Again, we find missing in Scotus—as in the rest of medieval theologians—an adequate biblical investigation of the problem. How much more cogent his arguments would have been if grounded on a positive-exegetical analysis! But then, would it not be unfair to hold this deficiency against him rather than against the age in which he lived? This shortcoming notwithstanding, it cannot be denied that Scotus' theology of the primacy is thoroughly biblical in its pivotal inspiration.[33] Nor can it be denied that in the history of this question of momentous importance for Christian theology, the Subtle Doctor adopted a stance remarkable for its solidity and brilliance.

3.
The Contribution
of the Theological Schools

The theological Schools were born in the Middle Ages and, by espousing a precise vision based on diverse spiritualities, philosophical perspectives, and theological tenets formulated by the great Masters, contributed to the organic development of fundamental principles and suggestions previously received. Their differences of opinion and their controversies served to render the various doctrinal aspects more lucid and exact.

Undoubtedly, together with their positive contribtuions, the theological Schools showed also some negative sides. A lack of originality fettered them; an excessive theological parochialism led them to radicalize divergent opinions and to embrace extreme positions without regard for nuances; they often reached a relentless crystallization of stands that rendered a fruitful dialogue impossible. Nevertheless, they faithfully conserved the substance of their inspiration, even though the love of subtleties and the effort to be distinguished from their "adversaries" at all costs frequently threatened to stifle their most fecund elements.

Concerning the doctrine of Christ's primacy, "Thomists" and "Scotists"—as they now will be called—have engaged in an acrid contest for centuries down to the present with almost unaltered positions. Francisco Suárez, S.J. (d. 1617) endeavored with his characteristic eclecticism to overcome tensions by inaugurating another "School." Since the respective positions have not changed appreciably, we need not follow the development of each School on our subject. Nevertheless, the debate does bring to light some new and explicit elements which we deem opportune to mention.

1. The Thomistic School

In general, the Thomistic School endorsed and commented on the solution proposed by St. Thomas. Some of its theologians, however, formulated the Thomistic viewpoint with divergent emphases. For example, it seems to us that Tommaso de Vio, O.P. (d. 1534), better known as Cardinal Cajetan, and the *Salmanticenses* in the seventeenth century indicated and underlined particular aspects of the Thomistic thesis, while the French Oratorian, Louis Thomassin (d. 1695) carried some principles to unacceptable extremes. His own "logic," however, disclosed how vulnerable his point of departure was.

At the time Cajetan wrote, the two opinions already had a precise and antithetical countenance. Thus, to the Scotists' mind, Christ is willed and predestined "before" every other creature; He is the center of the economy of salvation, and hence all things, whether natural or supernatural, have been created in Him and for Him. The Thomistic opinion, on the contrary, affirmed that Christ owes His existence exclusively to the sin of Adam; He was willed and predestined "after" the prevision of sin and only because of it.

In his defense of the latter viewpoint, Cajetan did not limit himself to the well-known reasoning of St. Bonaventure and St. Thomas, but finding himself confronted with Scotus' solution, he sought to emasculate it by endeavoring to show its inconclusiveness.[1]

2. Cardinal Cajetan's Solution

Already in the introduction of the question, Cajetan seems to part company with St. Thomas in a significant way. Whereas the Angelic Doctor states that there are two answers to the concrete problem, and that he selects the second as the more probable, Cajetan holds that two solutions are possible, namely, one which regards pure possibilities (and this would be Scotus' solution), and a second one which takes into consideration effective reality (the Thomistic solution). As we have repeatedly pointed out, however, for the theologians of the Middle Ages, it was not a question of distinguishing between possibility and reality, but of two interpretations of the concrete order of the Incarnation. For the rest, in the form proposed by Cajetan the question admits of absolutely no possibility of discussion, for who has ever denied that the Incarnation was possible abstracting from the circumstance of sin? But let us ignore this tendentious presentation of the *status quaestionis* and examine the author's critique of Scotus' basic arguments.

Cajetan notes that in the effective reality of the present universe there are three distinct orders: The order of nature, the order of grace, and the hypostatic order. Speaking properly, he says, the order of nature is the object of divine Providence; the orders of grace and the hypostatic order are objects of predestination *sensu proprio*. Hence, when we refer to predestination, we must have in mind only the last two orders, not the first. Now, the three orders are not only distinct, but historically they have a separate existence. This assertion is the key to the solution suggested by Cajetan. God first created the order of nature which was the object of divine Providence; with its own natural structure and finality, the *ordo purae naturae* is the beginning of history. On this is superimposed, by God's free will, the order of grace, which is the object of divine predestination. Cajetan is speaking of a grace without reference to Christ, a *gratia Dei*. Thus man and the universe, which were already constituted as nature, receive a new structure and finality which is supernatural. Finally, after Adam's sin, and in order to repair it, God decrees the Incarnation. In this fashion a third order, the hypostatic, is superadded, and the two preceding orders automatically assume a Christological structure and finality. Christ now becomes the Head of all creation.[2]

It is obvious that in the above elaboration, Cajetan harks back to the three parts of St. Thomas' *Summa*.

Now the author inquires: To which of the three orders does sin belong? And his answer is: Undoubtedly to the order of nature, since to sin is proper to man, not to grace.[3] This being so, Cajetan concludes that Scotus' argument based on predestination collapses: " . . . patet falsam esse Scoticam imaginationem." Indeed, predestination is related to the order of grace, which presupposes Providence, i.e., the order of nature to which sin belongs. In fact, Cajetan widens the distance between Christ and sin by inserting the order of mere grace between the order of nature and the hypostatic order. For the author, therefore, it is absurd to say that Christ was willed "before" sin:

> Cum peccata pertineant partim ad ordinem naturae et partim ad ordinem gratiae ut opposita illi, consequens est quod praedestinatio Jesu Christi ut sit Filius Dei praesupponat praevisionem futurorum peccatorum utpote spectantium ad praesuppositos ordines *in genere causae materialis*.[4]

Having thus "unhinged" Scotus' primary argument, Cajetan tackles the second, namely, the one based on the *ordinate volens*. Here, however, he finishes off the matter with dispatch. After a few distinctions on which everyone agrees, he states: God could have willed Christ before all creatures, but Sacred Scripture tells us that *de facto* God willed Christ on account of sin. And so, the question is closed:

> Nos enim, quia ex Scriptura non habemus incarnationem nisi redemp-
> tivam, dicimus quod—licet potuisset Deus velle incarnationem etiam
> sine redemptione futuram—de facto tamen noluit eam nisi sic; quia
> ipse non aliter revelavit suam voluntatem, quae ex sola ipsius revela-
> tione cognosci potest.[5]

There is no comment on the last statement. After all, if it is truly the teaching of Revelation that God became man exclusively in order to redeem us from sin, then of course the case is closed. But one suspects that not even Cajetan himself is too sure of this, for he tries to show at length that the theological arguments of Scotus are not convincing.

The judgment which Cajetan's presentation has evoked in certain quarters has been rather harsh and resentful. For instance, the Dominican savant, Ambrose Catarino (d. 1553), who on this question dissents from the Thomistic School, makes the following observation:

> Hoc autem Cajetani commentum vere adeo falsum esse existimo ut, salvo honore qui illi debetur, non ducam dignum quod ad disputationem ponatur. . . . Ego vero vix adducor ut super hujusmodi considerem; sed propter eos qui putant esse oracula, suscipiendus est labor.

And he characterizes Cajetan's elucubrations as being "monstrous," dictated by sectarianism, a total distortion of St. Thomas' teaching on predestination.[6]

Suárez, substantially agreeing with Catarino's judgment, noted ironically that, according to Cajetan's theory, one would have to say that God foresaw the sins of Christ's crucifiers and of the Anti-Christ "before" He foresaw Christ Himself, inasmuch as sin belongs to the order of nature, which is the first willed.[7]

Father Risi, who devoted several decades to the study of this question, defines Cajetan's solution as chimerical, capriciously invented, leading to absurdities, great blunders, and outrageous nonsense of various kinds.[8]

These acrid observations were of course provoked by the glaring flaws and incongruities of Cajetan's solution. The radical deficiency is found in the fact that the author presents the order of historical priority ("ordo executionis") as coinciding and identical with the order of intention ("ordo intentionis"). Since the notions of man, nature and creation precede the notions of grace and of Incarnation (God-Man), Cajetan concludes that the former precede the latter also historically and in the order of values. In other words, since God "first" created man and "later" elevated him to the supernatural order (at least with a logical posteriority), and finally, after the Fall, the son of God became man, Cajetan deduces that God, in His design, followed the same order of succession, adding a new decree after the preceding one had been carried out.

Note also that the order of pure nature to which Cajetan has recourse has never existed; it is mere conceptual hypothesis. An order which never existed could not have been foreseen by God as existing. The author obviously confuses and identifies the ambit of the *scientia simplicis intelligentiae* (which regards possibilities) with that of the *scientia visionis* (which refers to really existing beings).[9]

A similar observation must be made concerning the order of grace without Christ. The world was raised to the supernatural order from the beginning, but that order was not an anonymous reality, that is, without Christ. An order of grace abstracting from Christ has never existed, although it is *per se* possible. As St. Paul teaches, "God has elected us in Christ before the creation of the world" (Eph. 1:4). It is in Christ that "all things were made in heaven and on earth. . . . He is the firsborn of all creatures and all things subsist in him" (Col. 1:16-17). He is "the only mediator [of grace] between God and man" (1 Tim. 2:5).

Finally, from Cajetan's theory we would have to conclude that the universe has changed finality three times in its history. First, it had a purely natural finality (*ordo purae naturae*); later, that end was replaced by a supernatural finality (*ordo gratiae*), and lastly, through the Incarnation, Christ *became* the third end of creatures. How can we characterize these finalities thus cemented together? Either they will remain wholly extraneous to creatures, or else we will have to say that the universe has totally changed every time a new end has been superadded.

The mechanism introduced by the distinguished Cardinal in connection with the relation of nature to supernature had vast and not very felicitous consequences in subsequent theology. Limiting ourselves to our specific question, we may call attention to yet another incongruity: Before and after the Fall, Adam has two different supernatural finalities. He finds himself, then, in two different orders, the second of which is much higher than the first; and he owes the "progress" to his own sin, without which he would never had reached the second!

But we need not point to all the absurdities that follow from the author's thesis; he himself accepts them quite calmly:

> Neque est absurdum Deum prius praevidisse casum Adae quam praedestinasse Christum; sicut non est absurdum Deum praevidisse

leporem cursurum et *monstra futura* [what a dismal imagination!] et reliqua ad naturae ordinem spectantia quam praedestinasse Christum.[10]

In order to arrive at the heart of the problem it suffices to note that Cajetan never seems to care for the well-known principle, "Finis ultimus in exsecutione, primus est in intentione." It is exactly this axiom that constitutes the theological soul of Scotus' "ordinate volens." We are dealing here with a principle so evident that no one ever questioned it. St. Thomas himself makes it one of the pivots not only of theology but of metaphysics as well. The end, which is last in the order of execution, dominates the whole process from the beginning; it qualifies it; it characterizes it and renders it intelligible. In the words of the Angelic Doctor: "Finis inter alias causas primatum obtinet, et ab ipso omnes aliae causae habent quod sint causae in actu; agens enim non agit nisi propter finem."[11] The end preordains and organizes the various moments of the process of execution. Although these precede structurally and chronologically, they are always for the sake of the totality which is constituted by the end.

From the indisputable fact that the end or purpose of the salvific plan is concretely nothing else but eternal life *in Christo*, it follows that Jesus Christ as Head was willed and foreseen by God "before" all other creatures, inasmuch as He is the permanent source of their blessedness. The end is what determines the existence and the actions of all the intermediate causes, as Aquinas correctly insists.

Scotus' argument based on predestination, and the one on the *ordinate volens*, do nothing but make explicit the relationship between the end and the moments that lead to it. Cajetan, on the contrary, destroys the unitary movement of the salvific plan; he introduces three stages, three finalities, three orders, and projects the succession of the sphere of execution into the sphere of intention.

Cajetan's perspective—which, incidentally, embodies the substance of the Thomistic position[12]—makes it clear that we are face to face with a radical outlook which affects the entire realm of theology. In it, Christ appears simply as a *means*, as an instrument willed by God in subordination to the needs of sinful mankind. Anthropocentrism and hamartiocentrism emerge as the indispensable background of the mystery of salvation and the governing values within which the Incarnation finds its meaning.[13]

It is very difficult to see how this theory can be harmonized with the teaching of Sacred Scripture, especially that of St. John and St. Paul, according to whom both the *reditus in Deum* and the *exitus a Deo* are thoroughly Christological and Christocentric.

3. The "Corrections" of the Salmanticenses

The most obvious—and the greatest—difficulty created by Cajetan's solution is its merely external superimposing of one order over the preceding one, particularly in the case of Christ. Conceived as a "means" of restoring a pre-existing order, Christ does not form an integral part of it; He is not vitally inserted into it; He is extraneous, extrinsic to it. The dualism "nature-grace," "world-Christ" is rigorously rooted in Cajetan's thought with all the consequences that flow from it in the theological field.

The *Salmanticenses*, the celebrated Carmelite theologians of the University of Salamanca in the seventeenth century, and most faithful disciples of St. Thomas, became aware of the vulnerable point in Cajetan's theory and sought to remedy it, thus enhancing the Thomistic tradition on our question with new clarifications.[14] And the "corrected" presentation proved so satisfactory that it managed to dominate the field almost completely down to the present time. By exploiting the observations and subtle distinctions of the *Salmanticenses*, Thomists were actually enriching their thesis by assimilating whatever they thought valuable in Scotus' presentation, although retaining the integrity of their patrimony on the subject.

The *Salmanticenses* begin by noting that they are confronted with two fundamental statements which seem to them equally valid and beyond discussion.

The *first* is the one which constitutes the heart of the Thomistic position: "If Adam had not sinned, Christ would not have come." According to them, this is not an opinion but a most certain thesis, since Sacred Scripture and the Fathers teach it in an unequivocal and indubitable way. They point out that when the end is missing, the means to the end are not chosen. Thus, if Adam had not sinned, God would not have had the "motive" to decree the Incarnation. The reasoning is diaphanous: Christ is the *means*, and the sin to be repaired is the *end*. Since the means is subordinated to the end, God foresees sin first, and then Christ.[15]

The *second* statement—equally beyond discussion—is taken by the *Salmanticenses* from none other than Scotus, whose reasoning on the *ordinate volens* they dutifully appropriate as follows: Jesus Christ, "exigente excellentissima ejus dignitate," *must* have been "primum volitum et intentum a Deo per modum *finis cujus gratia* permissionis peccati, reparationis humanae et ceterarum rerum." God could not have willed that which is greatest for the sake of that which is inferior. Christ, therefore, has a right to a primacy of finality over all creatures, and so He must have been the first to be willed by God.

While Cajetan thought that Scotus' arguments were only sophisms, and not very clever at that, the *Salmanticenses*, themselves loyal disciples of St. Thomas, regarded them as sufficiently weighty to establish an indisputable certainty. According to our Carmelite theologians, it cannot be denied that Christ, owing to His intrinsic dignity as God-Man, was the end of all things and was, therefore, the first to be willed.

But can these two radically opposed perspectives be reconciled? Although the history of theology had given a negative answer, our authors are confident that it can be done. The key to their solution is provided by the distinction between *finis cujus gratia* and *finis cui*.

The *finis cujus gratia* of the Incarnation is that final purpose intended by God to dominate the whole and for the sake of which all other works and realities are willed. In our case, this end *cujus gratia* is the intrinsic excellence of the mystery. The *finis cui* of the Incarnation is man in need of redemption because of Adam's sin. The first end (*finis cujus gratia*) is an end in the full and strict sense. The second (*finis cui*) is an end in an improper sense, "in ratione causae materialis." The two ends are connected in the Incarnation in such a way that "Incarnatio esset prior in ratione finis cujus gratia quam nostra salus; haec vero esset prior incarnatione in genere finis cui et in ratione causae materialis."[16] In other words, the first thing willed by God was either the Incarnation *or* man's redemption, depending on the viewpoint from which we consider the matter. But some further precisions are necessary.

We can ignore the remarks of the *Salmanticenses* concerning the "signa rationis" used by theologians to describe the various priorities. They themselves maintain that there are only two "signa": one for the divine intellect, and one for the divine will. If this were true, the very possibility of discussion would be precluded, since we would lack an instrument to understand the relationship of order among the various divine operations. Of course, the authors contradict themselves quite frequently; their lucubrations actually abound in "signa rationis."

As to the distinction between "finis cujus gratia" and "finis cui," we observe that it was not original with the *Salmanticenses*. The application to our problem, however, was relatively new. They say: as a "finis cujus gratia," Christ is the first to be willed; but when the "finis cui" is considered, Christ is willed "after" Adam's sin is foreseen. Up to here, nothing decisive.

But now we ask: Are these two finalities parallel, or is one to be seen as subordinated to the other? This is the crux of the problem. If they are parallel, we commit the absurdity of saying that Christ was willed "before" and "after" Adam's sin was foreseen, that is, both independently of it and in dependence upon it. If, on the contrary, one of the finalities is subordinate, then we will have either the Thomistic or the Scotistic opinion, but not a new solution.

Actually, the reasoning of the *Salmanticenses* is reducible to this: The instrinsic excellence of Jesus Christ determines His being willed first as the end of all creatures. But God wills Him also for the sake of our redemption. These two statements are so evident that they are accepted by all. However, as such, they say absolutely nothing that can solve the problem. They become relevant and significant only when we inquire into their mutual relationship. The *Salmanticenses*, of course, unceasingly maintain that sin is the *end, condition, cause,* and *motive* of Christ's existence.

Now, this is exactly where the problem lies: Since the connection between the Incarnation and sin is *extrinsic* (that is, it depends on God's will), the question is to determine, through an analysis of Revelation, whether Christ was willed by God *first,* and then all things dependent on Him, or whether God *first* willed the universe and man, *then* foresaw the sin of Adam, and *only then* predestined Christ.

It seems that, in the position adopted by the *Salmanticenses*, the "finis cui" becomes the *motive* of Christ's existence and is thus automatically transformed into a "fnis cujus gratia." Nor does it help at all to repeat, as they do, that (a) Christ is greater than all creatures, and (b) that He came to redeem us. These are two truths of faith which are not denied, and cannot be denied, by either group of contestants.

If, Christ's intrinsic greatness notwithstanding, He was willed as a "means"; if the redemption from sin was the "motive" and the *raison d'être* of the Incarnation, as the *Salmanticenses* hold, all the distinctions between "finis cujus gratia" and "finis cui" fail to throw any light on the subject. We end up with Cajetan's conclusion to the effect that, even though Christ was willed "after" the prevision of sin, He nevertheless *becomes* the end of all things on account of His intrinsic greatness.

The solution proposed by the *Salmanticenses* would make sense if it affirmed that the "finis cui" is wholly subordinated to the "finis cujus grata"; that is to say, if it affirmed, as the Scotistic School does, that God predestined Christ before everything else and independently of everything else, and that He wanted the salvation of all *in Christo Jesu.* But, of course, in this case sin no longer appears the motive or cause, or condition of the Incarnation.

Concerning the finalities of the *Salmanticenses*, adopted by other recent theologicans, the distinguished Jesuit, Paul Galtier, offers the following observation:

There is an effort here to introduce the theory of two mutual causes, each of which remains first in its proper order. But this consideration serves only to create confusion in this connection. It is all very well to say that when God wills a being made up of matter and form, the matter is willed as the material cause and the form as the formal cause. This truth has nothing to do with the consideration of the two plans which they endeavor to distinguish in the divine intention. In the order of intention, there is no other end truly utlimate than that being for whose sake something has been chosen. The chosen object can, of course, have in itself a value that has determined its choice, but to the extent that it has been chosen *for someone else and exclusively for someone else*, it has not been willed, de facto, except as a means. Consequently, Christ, even though judged as being in Himself superior to all things, once He has been willed only for the good of the human race, is not, in the divine intention, the proper end of that choice. On the contrary, the ends are, each in its proper order, the human race and the salvation assured to it by decreeing Christ.[17]

The judgment which Father Risi had already expressed in this connection was even more severe, but it was not less accurate and pertinent. According to this author, the system of the *Salmanticenses* is a medley of irrational ideas and conclusions. One of these conclusions would be, for example, that a being willed exclusively for a particular end, becomes, by mere title of fact, a universal end, while it would not have any reason to exist among the very beings whose end it is![18]

We conclude that the effort of the *Salmanticenses*, even with the colorations added to it by their recent followers, does not go beyond the schema suggested by Cajetan and does not represent any progress at all as far as our question is concerned.

4. The Radicalism of Thomassin

In the history of theology the French Oratorian Louis Thomassin (d. 1695) is known mainly as the successor and emulator of Denys Petau, S.J. (d. 1652). In his *Dogmata Theologica*—three solid volumes written in pompous but impeccable Latin—the author shows his uncommon talent in exploring the mind of the Fathers, placing this ancient heritage side by side with Scholasticism in order to obtain a broader and fuller synthesis of Christian thought. Thomassin, however, is hardly ever mentioned in connection with the subject of Christ's primacy. And yet, it seems to us that his importance for our subject should not be underestimated, since it was he whose extreme radicalism led the basic premises of the Thomistic thesis to their ultimate conclusions.[19]

For our author, the Thomistic position is most certain, not only because it is clearly taught in Sacred Scripture, but also because an Incarnation independent of the Fall would be incompatible with God's dignity and, therefore, impossible. In Thomassin's view, the solution proposed by Scotus is offensive to God's attributes, especially His sanctity and justice, and must be absolutely rejected. This is the originality of our author's contribution.

The Incarnation, he holds, is essentially an "exinanitio Verbi," a true *kenosis*: "Ipsa Verbi incarnatio et praedestinatio Verbi incarnandi nonnisi inanitionem et divini fastigii ad ima inclinationem primo et per se sonat."[20] Since the Incarnation involves a radical "humiliation" on the part of the eternal Word, it postulates a proportionate cause. This plausible cause is exclusively the redemption of the human race.

Let us overlook the alleged repugnance between an Incarnation independent of the Fall and God's wisdom; this view rests entirely on Thomassin's ontologism. He even states that an Incarntion, *Adamo non peccante*, would be absurd and offensive to man because it would imprison man's attention on God *as man*, thus hindering his direct view of God's divinity! If the Incarnation, *in statu innocentiae*, is perceived as irrational and harmful to God and man, as the author claims, we would have to say that in Heaven the vision of Christ's glorious humanity will be a grave impediment for the blessed inasmuch as it will "distract" their attention from the direct vision of God!

Again, according to the author, an Incarnation independent of the Fall would be totally repugnant to God's goodness. Only man's sin justifies the humiliation of God incarnate. And it is exactly in the redemptive humiliation that the goodness of God is splendidly revealed. The only true goodness is the one that is joined with mercy over another's misery. "Insolentissimum est ut haec audeat amor, nisi quo succurrat lapso, opem ferat desperato amico."[21] Mercy, then, is the supreme form of goodness. God can love us only with a perfect love, that is, with a merciful love; and this, of course, presupposes our sins.

5. Mercy and Goodness

Many Thomists, while not endorsing all the outrageous exaggerations of Thomassin, believe that the very root of the Incarnation is precisely God's mercy. Thus Garrigou-Lagrange: "In Thomism the Incarnation appears as the supreme event of the universe . . . which manifests God's free love toward us *per modum misericordiae*."[22] The same author has published an article entitled, *Motivum Incarnationis fuit motivum misericordiae*.[23] And the title L. Ciappi gave to his dissertation was: *De divina misericordia ut prima causa operum Dei*.[24]

According to Thomassin, an Incarnation independent of Adam's sin would be contrary, not only to God's wisdom and goodness, but to His justice as well. This is based on the well-known Anselmian theory that only a God-Man could offer condign satisfaction for sin. Thus, to admit an Incarnation "before" the prevision of sin would be equivalent to saying that God willed to sacrifice His glory without a proportionately grave deficiency on the part of man, and this would be offensive to His justice. This is the premise that leads to hamartiocentrism and the Thomistic theory.

In our considered judgment, this position is erroneous. In effect, the root of the process is God's goodness, not His mercy. Goodness and mercy are not synonymous. The Incarnation is not the means to conciliate divine justice and goodness, but the effusion of God's goodness wishing to communicate itself *ad extra*. We have already explained these basic affirmations. We must now illustrate briefly the difference between goodness and mercy, and point to a fundamental equivocation by showing that goodness is the root of both justice and mercy. It emerges clearly that the Incarnation is the supreme event of the universe which manifests God's free and sovereign love, namely, His goodness, and that this goodness of God—not His mercy— is the "prima causa operum Dei."

The divine goodness is the cause of the existence of all things. By loving, the will of God creates the objects of His love and produces them unconditionally, after the fashion of a total donation, without being "motivated" by anything whatever outside of God Himself. As the Angelic Doctor teaches: "The object of the divine will is His goodness, which is His essence. Hence, since the will of God is His essence, it is not moved by another than itself, but by Himself alone. . . ."[25]

Hence, the "movement" which terminates in the production of creatures is born *ab intrinseco* in God, that is to say, is born of the free and sovereign inclination of goodness to communicate itself; its only reason is God's free, independent, creative love. In a word, the love of God does not rest on any moving or conditioning factor extrinsic to God, nor on any extrinsic and presupposed "occasion." Again the Angelic Doctor is explicit on the point: "Hence, although God wills things apart from Himself only for the sake of the end, which is His own goodness, it does not follow that anything else moves His will, except His goodness."[26] No need to insist on the subject. It is necessary, nevertheless, to have an accurate concept of freedom so as to ascertain adequately the notion of creation and of divine communication *ad extra*.

Considered in its source, the creative love of God is immutable because it is identified with the divine nature itself. But how explain that not all created beings are equal even though the same goodness of God is the cause of the existence of all? Not from the viewpoint of the divine will, says St. Thomas, but from the viewpoint of the good that is willed, that is, created.

In this way we must say that God loves some things more than others. For God's love is the cause of goodness in things. . . . No one thing would be better than another if God did not will greater good for one than for another.[27]

In the *Sed contra* of his article, the same St. Thomas quotes the well-known text of St. Augustine:

God loves all things that He has made, and among them, rational creatures more, and of these, especially those who are members of His Only-begotten Son; and much more than all, His Only-begotten Son Himself.[28]

It follows that the greater a creature, the more it is loved by God. Hence, Jesus Christ, being the God-Man, must be loved by God with a love greater than that shown to any other creature or to the entire universe.

Conceptually, mercy differs from goodness. The latter communicates itself *without* a previous condition: while the latter involves a rectification of a previous condition, an expulsion of evil or of an imperfection. It involves, therefore, an ulterior intervention which presupposes goodness: "Mercy takes its name from denoting a man's compassionate heart for another's unhappiness."[29]

Unlike goodness, then, mercy presupposes an external impulse or occasion. God's mercy is shown to creatures that are *already* existing and affected by imperfection or by evil. The relationship between goodness and mercy is synthetically described by the Angelic Doctor as follows:

The communicating of perfections, *absolutely* considered, appertains to *goodness*, as shown above . . . ; in so far as perfections are given to things in proportion, the bestowal of them belongs to *justice*, as has been already said; in so far as God does not bestow them for His own use, but only on account of His goodness, it belongs to liberality; in so far as perfections given to things by God expel defects, it belongs to *mercy*.[30]

Mercy, then, is the ulterior expression of divine goodness in so far as it expels defects or evil from creatures, or inasmuch as it enriches the creature with gifts not demanded by nature. The radical distinction between goodness and mercy lies essentially in this: Goodness is a communication without preexisting conditioning factors; it is absolutely creative. Mercy, on the contrary, presupposes a pre-existing, "external" reason or occasion to be remedied or corrected. One cannot, therefore, make God's goodness coincide with His mercy, as Thomassin does. The goodness of God is at the source of all His actions and governs them all. Liberality, justice and mercy are "derivations" of God's goodness and they presuppose created nature as already constituted (in its ideal or concrete being) because they act over it, while goodness is pure and liberal communication of God *ad extra* without anything being presupposed. That is why God's goodness may be expressed abstracting from His Mercy.

But one cannot even hold that mercy is the "motive" of the Incarnation. We say, on the contrary, that God's goodness is the *primary reason* (not the motive) of the mystery. That is to say, the Incarnation is not "conditioned" or "motivated" by any factor on the part of any creature. God has willed it, not owing to His mercy, but because of His goodness, although in its actual realization He has implemented the notions of justice and mercy—understanding mercy as a superabundance of goodness.[31]

6. Revealing Terminology

The Thomistic opinion, even while granting that God's goodness is the "reason" and the end of the Incarnation, as it is of every other creature, holds that mercy is its precise foundation inasmuch as the sin to be repaired is its "condition," its "motive," its "occasion," its "reason." According to Garrigou-Lagrange:

> De peccato, ut peccatum est [Thomistae] dicunt quod fuit *occasio* Incarnationis, et de peccato, ut redimendum est, dicunt quod fuit causa vel motivum, vel ratio ac conditio sine qua non Incarnationis.[32]

And, as expressed by C. V. Héris:

> We are thus permitted to conclude that, to the extent that the divine intentions are known to us, the redemption of the human race emerges as the true motive for which God determined to will the Incarnation of His Son.[33]

> The only motives on account of which God could decide to will the Incarnation are: either His own glory in the most perfect way that will constitute the manifestation of His love; or the glory of Christ-Savior in whom the perfection of the universe will be consummated; or final-

ly, the redemption and salvation of men.[34]

The above text presents three hypotheses: the first acknowleges God's goodness as the predominant reason (i.e., the Scotistic opinion); the second is the pseudo-Scotistic (and untenable) view which makes Christ the "perfection" of the universe; and the third is, of course, the Thomistic thesis. The same author continues: "God, it is true, has permitted our fall, but at once the heart of God was moved on account of our misery. Our misery provoked His mercy and *His mercy decreed the Incarnation.*"[35] According to the above, the presupposition which "provoked" God's mercy *ab extrinseco* is sin, which in turn is variously referred to as a *cause, condition, motive, occasion, reason,* etc., as if these terms were all synonymous! But if we make mercy the basis of the Incarnation, a few inevitable consequences follow.

The first is that the Incarnation is seen as being *totally* for the sake of our redemption from sin. The end, in effect, subordinates to itself the whole process, all the intermediate moments. Now, to redeem is an act of the God-Man, and every operation presupposes a being. This being is always superior to its actions; it has a previous, pre-eminent and more extended value than its operations. Hence, to affirm that the redemption is the true *motive* of the Incarnation means to subordinate the whole to a part, the existence to the operation. Right reason and the hierarchy of being clearly tell us the very opposite. An operation is the means to the realization of a being from which it proceeds. Thus, for example, eating is for the sake of life, philosophizing is for the sake of the life of the spirit, never the other way around. There are no reasons to weaken this hierarchy in Christ; if anything, there are reasons to strengthen it even more.

The second consequence is that Christ is seen as willed by God for the sake of other creatures, to redeem man. That is to say, He becomes a "means" in relation to man. Both Héris and Garrigou-Lagrange, quoted above, insist that our liberation from sin is the *end, motive, reason,* and *condition* of the Incarnation. If these terms mean anything, they mean that Jesus Christ was willed as a "means" to fulfill an end, namely, our liberation from sin, and this end governs and dominates "omnia quae sunt ad finem," and hence also Jesus Christ.

We say it again and again: To portray Jesus Christ, the most excellent of divine works, as a "means" to bring about our redemption, and therefore, as subordinated to it—this is a preposterous overturning of values that neither Cajetan's cleverness nor the dialectical arabesque of others will ever manage to camouflage. This is repugnant not only to right reason, but also—and directly—to Sacred Scripture. Christ is, in effect, God's "Beloved" *par excellence* (cf. Mt. 3:17; 17:15; Mk. 9:7; Lk. 9:35). Jesus is, in other words, the object of God's goodness and love in a unique, incomparable and perfect way. If the universe, the angels and man are the fruit of God's *un*conditioned goodness and not of His mercy, then *a fortiori* the same must be said of Christ. No, Christ does not owe His existence to man; man and all creatures owe their existence to Christ (cf. Eph. 1:4ff.; Col. 1:15ff.) As Cardinal Pacelli (later Pope Pius XII) once wrote:

> Jesus Christ is God's masterpiece, the greatest of His works, and whatever the moment and the circumstances of His manifestation in time, He is *the first to be willed by God, and in view of Him were all other things brought into being.*[36]

To hold, as some do, that sin is the end, motive and cause of the Incarnation, but that God willed Christ first on account of his intrinsic excellence (i.e., the theory of the two finalities) involves a contradiction. Either Christ's existence is willed for us, or we are willed for Him. *Tertium non datur!*

Besides, it is repugnant to think that an infinitely wise God will subordinate that which is greater to that which is lesser. As St. Thomas puts it: "Semper imperfectum est propter perfectius, et pars ignobilior est propter nobiliorem."[37]

In an analogous context, St. Cyril of Alexandria (d. 444), in the footsteps of St. Athanasius (d. 373), developed the same argument against the Arians who held that the Word was willed by God for our creation:

> If the Arians say that the Son of God has been created so that God might create us through Him, let them see the profanity into which they fall. For in that case He [the Son] appears to be for our sake rather than that we were made for Him; then we are the work, while He is the instrument. . . . If then the Son has been created for us instead of we for Him, we are undoubtedly more noble than He. But this is absurd.[38]

The "problem" of the so-called "motive" of the Incarnation arises only when we regard mercy as the source of that mystery. If there had been no misery to remedy (note the hypothetical formulation), there would not have been any need for mercy's involvement. The hypothetical formulation, then, is *essential* to the Thomistic theory. In the Scotistic position, on the contrary, the Incarnation results from God's goodness wishing to communicate itself in Christ in a supreme manner, and through Christ to all creatures. This position excludes both the hypothetical formulation (although many Scotists employ it as an explanatory device), and also the search for a "motive" of the mystery. Of course, through the Incarnation, God carries out His overall plan and enriches His creatures with many goods. He gives them their existence, grace, redemption, glory; He gives sanctifying grace to the angels, to innocent Adam, to Mary most holy. But Christ, having been willed on account of the divine goodness and not on account of mercy, has not been constituted a *means* to obtain all these blessings. These blessings are *not* the end or purpose of His existence; they are rather benefits flowing from the Incarnation. Christ, then, is not the means but the principle of diffusion, the source from which all receive, the center on whom all converge.

Just as God, by creating, does not become a "means" in relation to the creature receiving the benefit of creation (since to create means to communicate out of love, out of free, unconditioned goodness), so Christ's primacy is a source of enrichment and salvation for all without being subordinated to anything.[39]

To regard the divine goodness or the divine mercy as the foundation of the Incarnation means to choose between the two theological positions— Scotistic and Thomistic. As understood by the Franciscan School, the universal primacy of Christ is governed by God's goodness, thus neatly summarized by the Subtle Doctor:

> God first loves Himself; secondly, He loves Himself for others, and this is an ordered love; thirdly, He wishes to be loved by the One who can love Him in the highest way—speaking of the love of someone who is extrinsic to Him; and fourthly, He foresees the union of that nature which must love Him with the greatest love even if no one had fallen.[40]

7. The Position of Contemporary Thomists

In recent decades we have witnessed a renewed interest in the centuries-old controversy. It becomes ever clearer that we are dealing, not with a marginal problem, but with one of the most fecund and decisive foundations of the theological discipline.

Contemporary Thomists, while strictly adhering to their traditional stance (i.e., no sin, no Incarnation), have endeavored to broaden the horizon and to adapt to their synthesis the capital element of the Scotistic thesis, namely, the doctrine of the universal primacy of Christ.[41] Actually, this is not an altogether new effort. The *Salmanticenses*, for example, among others, had formally advanced it.[42]

As far as the terminology goes, there is no longer any Thomist who does not attribute to Christ a "primacy," indeed, a "true" primacy. According to Father Féret, O.P., Christ's primacy is "a datum of faith, prior to any particular theology. It is an elementary certitude of Christianity."[43] And Garrigou-Lagrange admits that, in the Thomistic position, "Christ holds the primacy of perfection . . . in the order of final, efficient and exemplary cause."[44] In the judgment of Father Bouëssé, O.P., "It is impossible for all of God's works not to have been ordained, in the first and only intention of His universal Providence, to the exaltation of the divine masterpiece [Jesus]."[45]

Does the above represent a massive abandonment of Thomism?[46] The terminology used would suggest an affirmative answer; but the reality hidden behind the words tells us a different story.

Trying to harmonize the essential thesis of Thomism (i.e., no sin, no Incarnation) with the Scotistic teaching on the absolute primacy of Christ would be the same as "wishing to unite water with fire," as Bonnefoy declares.[47] And Father Hugon, O.P., referring to the endeavor undertaken by the *Salmanticenses*, remarks: "They struggle hard . . . to prove that in this [Thomistic] theory, too, Christ can be called, in a legitimate sense, the center of creation and the firstborn of all the predestined."[48]

Note that they "struggle hard" to prove that "in a legitimate sense. . ." That means that there is also an illegitimate, captious, loose and improper sense to the universal primacy of Christ. It is precisely by attaching this illegitimate meaning to the primacy that recent Thomists can convince themselves of having successfully joined fire and water. But surely, no equivocation in terminology is going to resolve the problem. As long as one embraces the basic Thomistic thesis (i.e., sin is the cause of Christ's existence), an authentic doctrine of the primacy is simply impossible; it would be subjected to so many restrictions and contortions that it would emerge bleak and reduced to a skeleton.

Speaking concretely, we know that the universal primacy of Christ is carried out through the following threefold causality: exemplary, meritorious (efficient), and final. Under each of these aspects the primacy of Christ becomes practically an empty statement in the writings of the Thomists.

According to them, Christ's *exemplary* causality does not extend to Adam in the state of innocence, nor to the angels, nor to the order of creation. The same must be said of the *meritorious* (secondary, efficient) causality.

The Thomistic School unanimously denies that the elevation of our first parents to the supernatural life was due to the merits of Christ. The majority of its representatives, guided more by the logic of the system than by the authority of the Master [St. Thomas] and of Tradition, equally refuse to attribute the grace and glory of the angels to the merits of Christ. For the same reason, and contrary to the formal teaching of the *Summa* of St. Thomas and of the catechism of the Council of Trent, the angels are excluded from the Mystical Body of Christ.[49]

Let us listen to the way Garrigou-Lagrange echoes the Thomistic position: "Christus ut homo non fuit Caput primorum parentum innocentium quoad essentialem gratiam."[50] The reason is always the same: God willed Christ "after" the prevision of sin and only as Redeemer; hence, innocent Adam, having no need of redemption, had no relation whatever to Christ. The same holds for the good angels: "Christus ut homo non influit in angelos essentialem gratiam et gloriam."[51] The reason is the same as before. The author admits that Christ is the Head of the angels, but only inasmuch as they owe Him an "accidental grace." And he tries to show why this is sufficient:

> Nec est necesse ut caput morale angelorum influat in eos essentialem gratiam, nam ipsum caput naturale non influit in membra vitam essentialem, in actu primo, quae provenit ex anima tamquam a forma substantiali, sed solum aliquem motum vitalem in actu secundo.[52]

This is a very strange way to reason, really. The metaphor of the body was never dissected biologically in this fashion! For the rest, and to follow the same reasoning, we would have to say that Christ is the Head of men accidentally only, "nam caput naturale non influit in membra vitam essentialem."

As to the *final* causality, it too is subjected to the same distinctions and contortions. The Thomists affirm that Christ is the final cause of redeemed man *qua redeemed*; however, the order of creation, the angels and Adam do not have in Christ their original end, only their *acquired* head and end. Yes, everything has been "ordained" and oriented to Christ, but . . . only *after* the prevision of sin and redemption. In other words, in the beginning, nothing had Christ as an end; "later" everything was ordained toward Him. But this is equivalent to denying the universal finality of Christ because, as we have already noted, no one can in any way *become the end* of an order which already has an end; that involves a metaphysical absurdity. As an *acquired* end, Christ would always be extrinsic and marginal to the universe—an afterthought, so to say.[53]

8. A Telling Example

The dense volume published not long ago by Emilio Sauras, O.P. under the title *El Cuerpo Místico de Cristo*, is highly significant in connection with the effort of present-day Thomists to insert Christ's universal primacy into the old framework.

According to the author, a true primacy of order and of finality over all creatures is due to Christ. "No theologian or theological School questions it, although not all agree on the manner of explaining it."[54] A little later, however, he notes that when St. Paul speaks of Christ's supremacy as beginning and end, the reference is sometimes to the God-Man, sometimes to the eternal Word, prescinding from the Incarnation.[55] The texts cited by Sauras are Col. 1:15-20; Eph. 1:20-22; and Rom. 8:29. In our opinion, it is very difficult to hold, from an exegetical viewpoint, that the Apostle is here speaking of Christ *as God*, unless we wish to do violence to the text in an illogical and capricious fashion.

Having established the general proposition concerning the universal primacy, the author inquires whether it is something preordained by God or rather something contingent on the prevision of sin. Sacred Scripture, he answers, has two series of texts. The first series "clearly affirms that Christ is the Head of all creation, the beginning and the end of everything, prior to everything and in whom everything finds its explanation." But there is also another set of texts "in which it is affirmed that the existence of Christ depends on a concrete purpose: the redemption of man."[56]

Evidently, the two scriptural theses cannot be contradictory. There must be a way to reconcile them. But how? The author accomplishes it by subordinating the Incarnation to the reparation for sin—the Thomistic position. "The Scriptures make clear to us in many ways that the redemption of men is the *determining motive* of the Incaration."[57] It is precisely through the redemption that Christ becomes the beginning and the end of pre-existing creation. He is willed "after" the prevision of sin, and if He is said to be the Head of every creature, it must be understood as a tardily superimposed and superadded Head.

But if the reparation of Adam's fault is the *exclusive* reason why God became man, what becomes of the universal primacy of Christ which, on Sauras' admission, is clearly taught in Sacred Scritpure? How can hamartiocentrism be brought into harmony with Christocentrism? The author solves the problem by resurrecting the theories proposed by Cajetan and the *Salmanticenses* and already known to us.[58] However, his brave attempt yields nothing but a *purely verbal* affirmation of Christ's primacy. Furthermore, when Sauras tells us that the grace of the angels and of innocent Adam was not a *gratia Christi*, and then assures us that, according to St. Paul, Christ is "the beginning and the end of everything, hence also of the angels and of all the graces of the angels,"[59] is he not guilty of a flagrant contradiction? The whole affair is nothing but a desperate struggle to harmonize incompatible theories.

9. Concluding Remarks

At the end of this brief exposé of the Thomistic position, we must confess that it is unacceptable in its substance because it cannot be brought into conformity with the doctrine of Christ's primacy which is the very heart of the mystery of salvation. This sentiment, incidentally, is shared also by numerous non-Franciscan theologians.[60]

In contemporary Protestant theology, which rejects the *magisterium* of the Church and clings exclusively to Sacred Scripture, Christocentrism is quite generally proclaimed as the very essence of divine Revelation. Subsequently we shall recall the teaching of Karl Barth relative to Christ's primacy as the center of Christian theology. There are many non-Catholics who endorse this opinion. We may mention, for example, Prof. H. W. Schmidt who, having studied both viewpoints, comes to the conclusion that the Scotistic thesis is in perfect agreement with Scripture, while the Thomistic hamartiocentrism is simply unacceptable.[61] And in Oscar Cullmann's judgment, it is only in Christ that the mystery of salvation is condensed; it is only in Christ that we find the ultimate explanation of all that exists in Heaven, on earth, and in the lower regions.[62]

As regards the theology of the Orthodox, it harks back to the great tradition of the Greek Fathers who see man's "deification" and the "physical" theory of the Incarnation as the essence of Christianity. In this perspective, which is eminently Christocentric, the doctrine of the universal primacy finds its root, its most signal foundation.[63]

Should we, therefore, reject every aspect of the Thomistic position?

While we do not accept either the theory's formulation or its basic thesis or the reasoning behind it, we admit that one of its elements constitutes a positive contribution to the theological study of Christ's primacy and hence should not be overlooked. We have in mind the Thomists' vigorous assertion that Incarnation and Redemption cannot be conceived as issuing from *two* decrees in such a way that the former (Incarnation) is foreseen and willed by God "prior" to all things, while the latter (Redemption) was willed only after the prevision of the Fall. The Thomists correctly insist that the divine plan concerning Christ encompasses Him in His totality and in a unitary manner without the intervention of "breaks" or successive decrees. The Thomists rightly observe (against the majority of Scotists) that we can in no way speak of Christ's having been willed in an *impassible* flesh before the prevision of sin, and of Christ as willed *in carne passibili* after that prevision. The divine decree, then, must involve Incarnation *and* Redemption *per modum unius*; and also the Resurrection, let us add. This insistence, peculiar to the Thomistic School, is of the greatest importance for a correct understanding of the doctrine of the primacy. We shall see it in greater detail when we discuss the "Scotistic" position.

4.
The "Tertia Via" Proposed by Suarez (d. 1617)

The contribution which the Jesuit Francisco Suárez made to the doctrine of Christ's primacy was considerable indeed. This talented theologian was extraordinarily familiar with the theology of his predecessors. He knew how to evaluate accurately the various positions encountered, and although influenced by that eclecticism for which he has often been reproved, he was able nevertheless to imprint his own personality on every problem he confronted.

The author's views on our subject are propounded extensively in his lengthy treatise *De Incarnatione*,[1] and also in some of his subsequent writings.[2] He does not regard our question as a marginal, idle debate; it constitutes, on the contrary, the basis for two general perspectives on the entire theological panorama. In this respect, Suárez rises like a giant above all the other theologians who discuss this topic.

Having illustrated the fittingness of the Incarnation, the author proceeds to the problem "De primaria causa et ratione propter quam Incarnatio praedestinata et facta est, et sine qua non fieret." He begins by establishing the need to admit, in the divine intellect and will, an "ordo quidam secundum prius et posterius," that is, certain moments or "signa," although, of course, in God "illi actus aeterni sint et omnino simul."

> Licet enim Deus unico et simplicissimo actu omnia intelligat et velit, tamen quia inter scientiam et voluntatem et inter res ipsas cognitas vel amatas, est quaedam connexio et dependentia, ad hanc explicandam concipimus nos unum in divina mente et voluntate ut prius et posterius alio; et hoc modo distinguuntur in his actibus priora et posteriora non

secundum rem sed secundum rationem. Et hoc sensu explicatus ordo hic a nullo theologo negatur et illo saepe utitur S. Thomas.[3]

Having set down the above necessary premise, Suárez presents the problem in its classical terms: "Utrum voluntas Incarnationis antecesserit in Deo praescientiam originalis peccati vel subsecuta fuerit." After explaining successively the two well-known positions, he refers to a third one (his own), through which he seeks to harmonize the first two.

Of the two preceding solutions, Suárez adheres to the Scotistic one with his usual sagacity. His demonstration is characteristic especially because of the richness of biblical and patristic documentation. Passing on to the theological argument, the author proves that God willed the Incarnation independently of Adam's sin, and concludes:

> Deum non voluisse hoc mysterium solum quia occasio peccati oblata est ut praecognita, *sed potius e contrario*, ideo permisisse peccatum ut ex illo occasionem sumeret optimo modo se communicandi hominibus.[4]

The above is based on the fact, generally accepted by theologians, that election and predestination to glory precede the permission of original sin. Since Christ was the greatest of the predestined, He was predestined not only before the prevision of sin, but even before the angels and men were predestined.[5]

The author's reasoning is, of course, borrowed from Scotus. Note, however, the connection which our author establishes between the Incarnation and sin. The Fall, he points out, was permitted by God as an *occasion* to communicate Himself to man *in a most perfect way*. Obviously, this situation would not exist in a world without sin. To Suárez, this is a grave and basic assertion; to Scotists, it is unacceptable.

More specifically, Suárez states that the *primary reason* for the Incarnation was the intrinsic excellence of the mystery itself and other benefits flowing from it, abstracting from sin.[6]

One of the decisive proofs of the thesis, according to Suárez, is the fact that the angels and innocent Adam owe their grace and glory to the merits of Christ. Since the grace of innocent Adam and that of the angels had been foreseen "before" the prevision of sin, *a fortiori* was Christ their Head so foreseen. The author corroborates the thesis with the authority of numerous Fathers and theologians, including the Angelic Doctor.[7] In his treatise *De Angelis*, written toward the end of his life, Suárez again expands on the subject.[8]

1. An Obscure and Fragile Point

After Suárez discusses the Scotistic solution, he formulates a fundamental query: Did God predestine Christ as redeemer through His Passion and death "before" the prevision of Adam's sin?[9] As we are already aware, this is the "crux," the greatest difficulty in connection with the Scotistic opinion. Suárez answers:

> Ante permissionem et propriam et absolutam praevisionem peccati, Christus *non* fuit praedestinatus ut redemptor, sed solum post peccatum permissum.[10]

The position adopted by Suárez does not differ, substantially, from that of the majority of Scotists who preceded him. But does the author not hold that, independently of the prevision of sin, the angels and innocent Adam owe their grace and glory to Christ? True, but Christ was willed as "glorifier" of the angels and of innocent Adam; in fact, even as their "Savior," if this term is properly understood.[11] For, even in the first moment of predestination, Christ may be said to have been foreseen as "Redemptor *quoad potestatem*, ut ita dicam, et *sufficientiam*" so that "ejus opera sufficientissima esse possent ad remedium, *si necessarium esset.*"[12] For the author, however, it remains true that the passibility and death of Christ had only one purpose, namely, to satisfy for our sins. Naturally, this narrow concept of Christ's death, dating back to St. Anselm, blocks the correct understanding of the Lord's absolute primacy. Besides, it overlooks an important value inherent in His death, which is primarily an act of the most perfect love and worship of God. In this respect, the author's horizon is dominated by anthropocentrism and hamartiocentrism.

The second grave deficiency, common to Suárez and other theologians, consists in limiting the notion of redemption exclusively to that of "liberation from sin." Suárez declares this as an absolute principle: "Nullus redimitur nisi is qui sub peccato servit."[13] From these premises he is forced to conclude: (a) that the angels were not redeemed by Christ; and (b) that the redemption, *sensu concreto*, necessarily presupposes sin and was willed "after" it, just as medicine presupposes illness.

Two very serious objections are raised against the above, and Suárez discusses them quite openly and fairly.

A) The first objection hinges on the notion of God's infallible will. According to the decree actually willed by God, Christ came *in carne passibili*. If God had willed the Incarnation "before" sin (hence, *in carne impassibili*), His will would have been carried out infallibly, since it cannot be hindered by any creature. Therefore, one must conclude that God did not wish Christ to come that way, not even *ab initio*.

Suárez answers: God willed an impassible Incarnation with an antecedent will; "voluntas enim antecedens aequivalet voluntati conditionatae." Hence, God "voluntate absoluta et efficaci voluit Incarnationem *tantum quoad substantiam* mysterii in hac Persona, in hac natura individua; modum autem ejus non definivit donec peccatum permissit et praevidit."[14] But we may ask: Does that answer solve anything? If God wills the Incarnation, He wills it not only *quoad substantiam*, but with all its concrete modalities; otherwise it is an absurd manner of willing on God's part. Besides, if we admit the validity of the distinction between the "substance" and the "modality", do we not have to conclude that a stupendous and marvelous reality like the death of the Savior depends on sin? And if so, are we not perhaps forgetting all the insurmountable difficulties we ourselves raised against the Thomists for holding that the Incarnation depended on the fall of our first parent? As we shall see, it is precisely to obviate this obstacle that Suárez will devise his "third way."

B) There is a second objection to be met. Suárez holds that Christ is the source of grace and glory for the angels, but not their Redeemer because they had not sinned. But could it not be said that Christ is their Redeemer by way of preservation? This is an opening that would have led to a radical solution. But Suárez answers that this opinion, although embraced by some, cannot be admitted:

> Nec satis est quod potuerint peccare et propter merita Christi praeservati sunt. . . . Hoc non sufficit ad propriam redemptionem quia redemptio dicit iteratam emptionem.[15]

It is true that St. Bernard and Denis the Areopagite explicitly teach that Christ redeemed the angels by preserving them from sin, but such assertions "non sunt omnino propriae et rigorosae . . . ; nos vero hic explicamus propriam et rigorosam significationem verborum."[16] This is the monotonous repetition of the axiom, "Nullus redimitur nisi is qui sub peccato servit."

But then it must be asked: In virtue of which merits did Christ sanctify the angels? Suárez answers: In virtue of those merits which Christ gained by means of the acts of charity which animated His life: " . . . gratia non est data angelis ex praevisione meriti fundati in morte Christi, sed fundati absolute in caritate et bonis operibus Christi hominis."[17]

It is remarkable that a theologian of Suárez's stature was able to make such statements. But the insuperable impasse to which he was driven by his narrow ideas concerning the extent of Christ's redemption and the value of His death left him no other way out. And the strange anomaly is this: Suárez, a fervent champion of the Immaculate Conception, followed Scotus' teaching to the effect that our Blessed Lady, though utterly sinless, was redeemed by Christ in a most perfect (preservative) manner. Why not apply to the angels the same principle that was valid in Mary's case?

In the second place, how can anyone hold that Christ merited for the angels with all the actions of His life *except* His death on the Cross? Does not every one of Christ's actions have, in the present economy, an internal orientation toward His death? The entire life of Christ is dominated by His death and resurrection. How can we separate His life from His death in the matter of meriting? How can the supreme expression of Christ's love—His death—be excluded in order to make room only for His "other actions"?

These questions illustrate the woeful inadequacy of Suárez's understanding of Christ's death. For him, it is only a "satisfactio de condigno." He thus overlooks its essential, biblically-supported value, namely, the Savior's worshipping love toward the Father conveyed by the all-encompassing surrender of Himself.

2. The Two Motives

The theological investigation undertaken by Suárez has not reached its culmination with the analysis of the two traditional opinions, nor with his manifest preference for the Scotistic viewpoint. The author believes it is most certain that the intrinsic excellence of the Incarnation is a sufficient and unconditioned motive for its realization. Nevertheless, he feels that there are other motives to be taken into consideration, such as, for instance, the perfection of the universe, the greatest communication of God's goodness, and man's redemption from sin. Of these, Suárez holds, the redemption is likewise a completely sufficient motive for the Incarnation:

> Motivum sufficiens et adaequatum volendi Incarnationem non fuit unicum, sed plura; non tantum partialia, sed totalia et per se sufficientia.[18]

It is not that the various motives coalesce into one single motive. Thus, both the intrinsic excellence of the mystery and man's redemption are autonomous reasons, sufficient and decisive, each in its order. The error of the two traditional opinions lies, according to Suárez, in assigning only one reason to the Incarnation. What we need is a synthesis of the two. It is in this connection that he introduces his own well-known solution:

> Tertia sententia media esse potest, quae utramque positam [the

Thomistic and Scotistic] quodammodo amplectatur; et primam rationem volendi hoc mysterium esse dicat tam excellentiam ipsius mysterii quam nostram redemptionem; ita ut in primo signo, quo Deus voluit hoc mysterium ex utraque ratione, tamquam ex quodam completo motivo, divina voluntas fuerit inclinata.[19]

Concretely, then, God willed the Incarnation for two distinct and independent reasons; each of these reasons would have been sufficient to "motivate" the decree. There is, nevertheless, a connection between the two sufficient motives, a connection with a bearing on the concrete order of things. Their autonomous validity, according to our author, must be situated at the level of divine knowledge which is the object of the "scientia media." That is to say: God sees in Himself the various possible worlds; the decisions of free causes in the divers hypotheses and circumstances; that which would happen in the various hypotheses; the concatenation of causes if placed in certain conditions. It is in this arrangement of the "scientia media" that the excellence of the Incarnation and the redemption appear as distinct motives, each fully sufficient, on God's part, to decree the Incarnation. There is no question here of pure possibles, but of hypothetical and conditioned possibles. The passage from hypothesis to reality takes place due to the free and gratuitous will of God, guided by divine wisdom. Still, the will of the All-wise God will bring to reality that hypothesis which will manifest, in one single indivisible act, the divine goodness, justice and wisdom *in the most perfect manner*.

Now, of the various hypothetical orders available, God chose the one that connects the Incarnation with sin to be repaired because only this order manifests the divine attributes *optimo modo*.[20]

Considering, then, the order of conditioned possibles (i.e., that of the "scientia media"), both Scotists and Thomists are correct; so Suárez declares. In effect, one can say that Christ would have come even if Adam had not sinned, and also that He came only to redeem us from sin; both motives are valid and sufficient by themselves to motivate the divine choice. If from the order of conditioned possibles we pass over to the concrete order actually willed by God, then the two motives co-exist simultaneously in the divine will. In the author's thought, his "third way" is the synthesis that conciliates the preceding thesis and antithesis. Nothing remains but to conclude optimistically:

In hac controversia, supposita sententia quam elegi et omnino veram existimo de modo praedestinationis Christi, vix intelligo posse esse dissentionem in ipsa re, sed fortasse in modo concipiendi et explicandi illam.[21]

3. The "Third Way" is an Illusion

The optimism expressed by Suárez concerning his own solution is not justified. Actually, there is no room for his "third way" between the preceding theories. It ends up by coinciding with one or the other. Between these two propositions: "God became man independently of sin," and its contradictory: "God became man because of sin," there is no possible middle space.[22]

When Suárez tells us that God *de facto* willed the Incarnation as a redemption from sin so as to carry out His plan "optimo modo," he is actually embracing the Thomistic thesis. And this, after having extensively demonstrated that the Incarnation was *not* contingent on Adam's fall!

A flagrant contradiction? It does not seem so. When Suárez favors the Scotistic opinion, he is speaking of a pure possibility, which no one has ever denied. But this is not *ad rem*, since our problem concerns, not the possible, but the real, concrete order. And as far as the real order willed by God is concerned, the two motives indicated by Suárez are not parallel and independent; one influences the other, and thus only one will be the determining factor. For Suárez, this determining factor is the reparation of sin, for it alone realizes the divine plan "optimo modo."

Even though the theory of Suárez practically coincides with the Thomistic theory (which he had so severely judged), his "tertia via" does not have the logic of Thomism when one accepts the latter's point of departure. In fact, the author sometimes falls into glaring contradictions. Let us mention a few.

The first serious observation concerns his manner of formulating the solution. He notes repeatedly that the choice of the concrete order in which the Incarnation is connected with Adam's fall has been dictated by the fact that God must act always "optimo modo." It seems that here Suárez falls into that metaphysical optimism which was later made famous by Leibniz (optimum ex parte operis). If so, he leaves himself wide open to all the criticisms which prove the absurdity of this system. If, however, the author has in mind (and this seems more likely) only the manner of acting in God (velle optimum ex parte operantis), then his demonstration is rather pointless, since God always acts in the most perfect (divine) manner, and does not act more perfectly in one hypothesis than in another. The whole Suárezian demonstration, then, rests on a very weak and unacceptable basis.

Turning now to the strictly theological argumentation, we observe the following: Suárez holds as theologically certain that the angels owe their grace and glory to Christ's merits, but not to those merits which the Savior acquired through His death. Now, in his "third way," all the merits of Christ are dominated by His death, inasmuch as God could not will the Incarnation except "optimo modo," that is to say, as a redemption from sin and, therefore, with Christ's death as the determining motive. We may ask: In virtue of which merits were the angels sanctified? In virtue of those "preceding" the death on the Cross and belonging to an Incarnation which abstracts from sin? But isn't such an Incarnation a pure possibility? Hasn't Suárez tried to prove that the only Incarnation that actually took place in the concrete order was an Incarnation that presupposes sins as a "conditio sine qua non"?

There is more. If the permission of sin is necessary for God to decree the Incarnation "optimo modo," one would have to say that sin is necessary for the perfection of the world as willed by God. But how can sin, which is something negative, contribute to the perfection of the universe, considering that perfection is something positive?[23] For the same reason, it must be said that God, who commanded Adam to avoid sin, did not really wish him to remain sinless because, having willed the Incarnation "optimo modo," He must have willed also the fall of our first parent.

The above contradictions must have troubled Suárez in later years. Eventually, and to his credit, he openly admitted that, despite his own efforts to prove that the Incarnation depended on the Fall,[24] he was not really convinced of that theory. Thus he wrote:

> Numquam illi sententiae assentire potui; et ideo censeo absolute quod, licet non fuisset Adam peccaturus, Unio Verbi in humana natura fieret, licet Redemptoris officium non assumeret.[25]

Notwithstanding the intrinsic weakness of the solution proposed in the "third way," it must be confessed that Suárez gave a notable impulse to a better understanding of Christ's primacy. This was due particularly to his having anchored the thesis in Sacred Scripture and patristic tradition. The Doctor Eximius had become, in fact, a common point of reference for all subsequent theologians, right up to the present time.

5.
The Scotistic School

In the course of so many centuries following the death of Blessed John Duns Scotus, the Scotistic School has added nothing of substance to what the Master had already propounded and championed. The task his followers undertook quite successfully was twofold: to defend Christ's primacy by showing the vulnerability of its adversaries' arguments, and also to develop the nucleus of Scotus' teaching in a harmonious fashion and according to all its virtualities. In more recent times a third task has been added with happy results, namely, to exploit the serious biblico-patristic studies of modern scholars and bring out the perfect agreement of the Scotistic position with bibilical and patristic thought.[1]

The first generations of Scotists, e.g., John de Bassoly (d. 1333), Peter of Aquila (d. 1370), Peter Aureoli (d. 1322), Francis de Mayronis (d. 1330) and Francis Rubió (d. 1333) simply restated the basic arguments of Scotus and added motives of fittingness borrowed from Alexander of Hales. Soon the Scotisitc position became widespread outside the Franciscan Order too, counting among its witnesses theologians of note like Denis the Carthusian (d. 1471) and Cardinal Nicholas de Cusa (d. 1464).[2]

The further development of the principles laid down by Scotus became manifest especially in the explicit application of the doctrine of the primacy to the area of the angels' grace and glory, and to the grace of Adam *in statu innocentiae*. Somewhat later, though not always explicitly, the cosmic implications of our thesis were likewise referred to.[3] But it is particularly the doctrine of Christ's universal Kingship, so deeply cherished within the Franciscan Order, that allows us to measure and evaluate this process of general application of Scotistic premises.[4]

Less felicitous was, at the beginning, the exposition of Sacred Scripture in relation to our theory. The primary argument of the Thomists to the effect that, according to the Bible, God had become man to redeem us, was simply met with the answer: Yes, that statement expresses a dogma of our faith that no one can deny. But it is not logical to equate a positive proposition with an exclusive one. From the fact that Sacred Scripture teaches that God became man to redeem us, it does not follow that He became man *only* or *principally* for that purpose. There does not exist any text either in Scripture or in the official documents of the Church to that effect. As to the thought of the Fathers, it was simply observed that one cannot be satisfied with some isolated passage; their position must be gleaned from the general context of their teaching. In more recent times, however, some serious studies have demonstrated that, as a whole, the Fathers of the Church are anything but favorable to the Thomistic theory.[5]

At first, then, the polemic with the Thomists did not yield a particularly valuable contribution to the field of positive theology. Following the custom of the times, the discussion was conducted mostly by dint of isolated citations rather than by trying to gauge the thrust of Revelation in its totality. We must note, however, that recourse to the famous text of the Epistle to the Colossians can be traced back to the earliest period. In subsequent times, the biblico-positive investigation undertaken led to a deeper conformity between the biblical and the theological exposition. Thus the great Scheeben, profound exponent of the Scotistic viewpoint, could write:

> Again, have we denied that the Incarnation is designed precisely to free fallen man from his sin, and that consequently God's love, which is the motive of the Incarnation, is a merciful love? We deny only that the wealth of this love is limited to the claims of compassion, and that the principle and motive of the Incarnation can be found in such limitation. This motive can be no other than the boundless love which God displays after man's sin, contrary to all expectation and beyond all our notions. And further, we deny that the elevation of fallen man was the only end or at any rate the highest end, and that love for man was the only motive or the highest motive of the Incarnation. The glory of Christ and of God Himself is the highest aim, and the love of God for Himself and for Christ is the highest motive of the Incarnation.[6]

In Scheeben's judgment, this is the essential teaching of Sacred Scripture and the Fathers. The Scotistic viewpoint not only "magis consonat judicio rationis [theologicae]," as St. Bonaventure acknowledged, but according to Scheeben, "plus consonat pietati fidei, quia auctoritatibus Scripturae et Sanctorum est magis conformis,"—which St. Bonaventure denied.[7] The exegesis and biblical theology of subsequent years have been a brilliant corroboration of Scheeben's judgment.[8]

Among those who in the post-Tridentine period contributed substanial-
ly to the spread of the Scotistic thesis, we may mention Bartholomew Mastri
(d. 1673), John de Rada (d. 1608), Claude Frassen (d. 1711), Philip Fabbri
(d. 1630) and Sebastian Dupasquier (d. 1705), all of them members of the
various branches of the Franciscan Order. Nor can we overlook the in-
valuable contributions of St. Bernardine of Siena (d. 1444) and the two Doc-
tors of the Church, St. Lawrence of Brindisi (d. 1619) and St. Francis de
Sales (d. 1622). In the more recent period, Matthias Joseph Scheeben
deserves a place of honor. It was he who treated the doctrine of the primacy
with rare sagacity and brilliance, coming to the conclusion that it was the
very center of Revelation:

> . . . scientific theology, if it is to apprehend Christ in all His meaning,
> must forge ahead to the point where it will consider Him as the center
> of gravity of the entire world order, and hence grasp the full sense
> of the words: "I will draw all thing to Myself."[9]

For Scheeben, the object of theology is the *Christian* mystery which has
its highest realization in Christ the God-Man. Hence

> . . . from every point of view our theological wisdom is bound up
> with the incarnate, personal Wisdom of God, is conformed to Him,
> and receives from Him its characteristic divine-human signature. Sub-
> jectively as well as objectively it is specifically Christian; for it is the
> science of the great mystery of Christ. . . .[10]

1. Two "Scotistic" Trends

After Scotus, the path of his doctrine was encumbered by polemics and
by undue adherence to individual viewpoints. It often intersected the parallel
doctrine of the Immaculate Conception, and even more frequently, the ex-
tenuating debates with the Thomists deflected attention from important
elements and shifted its focus to rather marginal questions.

In our previous explanation of the Thomistic opinion we sufficiently
recalled the salient aspects of the controversy, the objections it gave rise
to, and the respective rejoinders. It now remains for us to face a grave difficulty of the Scotistic position which created a cleavage among its adherents.
We are referring to the matter of a passible or impassible Incarnation. This
disunity defiled the thought of many theologians and hindered them from
drawing all the consequences from the principles laid down by Scotus.

What gave origin to the question was this: All Scotists agree on the basic datum that Jesus Christ, fruit of the love of God, was willed by Him "before" all creatures so that the entire universe is for Christ. Nevertheless, in the concrete realization of the divine plan, the Incarnation involves a redemptive mission and the mortal and passible condition of the human nature assumed by the Word. This poses the problem: Does the divine decree in its initial moment (*in primo signo logico*) already refer to the incarnate Word as passible and Redeemer, or do we have two decrees, the initial one concerning an impassible Incarnation, and a second one (after the prevision of the Fall) concerning a passible Incarnation? The first hypothesis would seem to lead to an intolerable consequence, namely, that sin must have been willed by God *ab initio*. (Note that this reasoning presupposes that "to redeem" means exclusively "to free someone from the slavery of sin.")

In view of this, the second hypothesis seemed the only plausible alternative. That is why the distinction between passible and impassible Incarnation became classic among some Scotists; in fact, the Scotistic opinion was generally known exclusively under this guise. But is this distinction compatible with the absolute primacy of Christ? Does it not involve a "change" in the divine design provoked by the creature's guilt? Doesn't this distinction lead us to admit some of the very inconveniences we reject in the Thomistic opinion? Is it faithful to the solemn principle of Scotus who, speaking of Christ in the concrete order willed by God, appeals always to the "ordinate volens," to God's unconditioned love, and to the absolute priority of Christ's predestination? Doesn't the distinction represent a capitulation to the Thomists, without possessing the logic of their system, considering that it rests on different premises? For example, for the Thomists, original sin is the reason for the Incarnation; for the Scotists who admit the aforementioned distinction, sin explains the redemption. Now, in both cases sin has a true causality in relation to Christ; it would be a motive of His existence, either essentially (Thomists) or modally (Scotists).

2. Christ "Impassible" and "Passible"

The objections raised by the Thomists against that distinction were well founded indeed. The Incarnation, considered in the abstract and without its concrete modality, is not feasible; God's efficacious decrees are not formulated *in confuso*. Some said, furthermore, that the distinction was entirely unknown to tradition. On this point, however, the objection was not so well founded, for the distinction was familiar to St. Albert the Great,[11] St. Bonaventure,[12] and St. Thomas.[13] Scotus, too, was acquainted with it, but only as a possible answer to an objection; it did not constitute a determining factor of his thought nor of his formulation of the primacy. For the

Subtle Doctor, as we have pointed out, Christ's primacy rests only on these solid grounds: (a) the nature of predestination; (b) the creative and unconditioned love-goodness-will of God; and (c) the hierarchy of created values.

The above principles have reference to the Incarnation as it was willed by God in the present economy, without any changes or modifications in His plan. According to Scotus, therefore, the first and independent object of the divine design is Christ *incarnate and passible*. There is no room here for any distinction between the substance and the modality of the Incarnation.

And yet, there were difficulties to be overcome. Redemption, it was said, presupposes the sin from which one is to be redeemed; hence, the *redemptive* formality of the Incarnation "follows" the prevision of sin. Sacred Scripture and the Fathers (the usual *auctoritates*) teach that the redemption was willed on account of sin. In the Scotistic tradition, therefore, the distinction became necessary, notwithstanding the principles which sustain the whole theological structure. Scotus' own answer is diffident; the distinction in question surely does not seem to be to his taste: "Omnes autem auctoritates possunt exponi sic, scilicet quod Christus non venisset ut redemptor nisi homo cecidisset, *nec forte ut passibilis*."[14]

That is to say, Scotus did not think it was impossible for Christ to come as He actually came (*in carne passibili*) even prescinding from sin. He mentions it as a problem about which he is not sure: "perhaps" Christ would have come in impassible flesh; but "perhaps" also He might have come in passible flesh—always regardless of sin. Redemption is, of course, undoubtedly connected with sin; in the Christian theological sense, to redeem means exclusively to free someone from sin.[15] In this wavering position of Scotus it is most important to note that, for him, it was not absurd, in fact quite in accord with his principles, that God should have willed, *in primo signo* and independently of everything, a God-Man *in carne passibili*.

The insoluble knot that caused his perplexity was the restricted meaning given to the term *redemption*. The solution, of course, could have been found in a broader and deeper notion of passibility and redemption.[16] That is why Scotus adheres to his "nec forte ut passibilis." Some of his first disciples[17] reveal to us that the Master's *tendency*, owing to his principles, was to hold that the object of the divine decree was precisely Christ as Head *and* Redeemer. They discarded the distinction between "quoad substantiam" and "quoad mondum" and had recourse to a very different distinction which allows them to speak of an independent predestination of the God-Man as Redeemer without thereby admitting a direct volition of the sin from which humanity was to be redeemed.

This new distinction is between *preservative* Redeemer and *liberating*

Redeemer. One cannot but sense here the obvious influence of the question then heatedly disputed on Mary's Immaculate Conception. Jesus Christ may be predestined as Redeemer independently of the prevision of sin, because He is a true Redeemer who *preserves* and *protects* from sin, who places finite freedom (of itself dominated by peccability) in a sinless condition. "In this case we would have a physician who prevents an illness, and not a physician who frees from an already contracted illness," as Peter of Aquila put it.[18] The recourse to the doctrine of the Immaculate Conception is here evident. Jesus Christ is Mary's Redeemer and Savior even though He did not free her from any sin, not even from the *debitum peccati* or the obligation to incur original sin. In fact, as Scotus had already brilliantly demonstrated, in Mary's case we have the most remarkable manifestation of Christ's mediatorial and redemptive power.[19]

In its deepest sense, therefore, *to redeem means to liberate a created freedom—by means of an elevation to the supernatural state—from a condition made possible by its peccability*. Thus, even if Adam had not sinned, Christ "venisset utique ut redemptor; non sicut modo, a peccato existente liberando, sed ab omni peccato quemlibet praeservando," as another disciple of Scotus writes.[20] Hence, when we say that Christ was willed as Redeemer *in primo signo*, it does not follow that the evil of sin was then willed as the *materia redimenda*. After all, the primary and essential object of Christ's redemption is the finite freedom, i.e., a freedom which is open to the possibility of sin. And, of course, the direct volition, on God's part, of a creature endowed with a finite freedom which is exposed to peccability is not at all incompatible with His sanctity. In this sense, redemption is essentially an effect of God's *goodness* (not of His mercy). In any case, the above perspective renders useless and empty the dangerous and untenable distinction between passible and impassible Incarnation.

3. St. Bernardine of Siena's Intuition

The thesis that Christ had been initially predestined as Redeemer with an absolute decree faced a second obstacle. *De facto*—so the objection ran—passibility and death are *deficiencies*, negative factors. As such, they could not have been positively willed by God as a concrete condition of the Incarnation; a privation cannot be the object of God's direct will.

Although only a few Scotists of the primitive period confronted the argument, St. Bernardine of Siena (d. 1444) knew the problem well and proposed a solution that is both sound and biblically supported.

Jesus Christ—the Saint explained—is the universal Mediator between God and all creatures. Angels and men make up the heavenly Jerusalem, whose Head is Christ. Following the Twelfth Chapter of the Apocalypse, St. Bernardine observed that the angels' decision (which rendered the faithful ones blessed and the others damned) had as its object the mystery of the God-Man. The faithful angels obtained their victory "by the Blood of the Lamb" (Apoc. 12:11), that is to say, through the merits of Christ's Passion. To the objection that the good angels had not sinned and hence could not have been admitted to God's friendship in virtue of the Savior's Blood, the Saint answered:

> Jesus Christ, the only Mediator, is Redeemer and Conciliator. He is called Redeemer because He perfectly satisfied to the Father for sin. He is called Reconciler, however, because He merited grace. Hence He was Redeemer of men who sinned and need the glory of God, because He satisfied for them through His most holy Passion. But He is the Reconciler of the angels because He merited grace for them. He was not Redeemer of the angels who did not sin, unless we take the word 'redemption' in a broad sense. Therefore, by virtue of the *same* merits of Christ were sinful men liberated from their sins and the angels preserved from sin.[21]

St. Bernardine, then, is faithful to the Scotistic position relative to Christ's primacy. The Savior was predestined *in primo signo* as God-Man Mediator, and this mediation, in the dynamic order, was carried out by means of the Passion and death on the Cross. The liberating influence of Christ takes on two different names depending on the object-terminus. It will be called "redemption" in relation to sinful man, and "conciliation" as regards the angels who did not sin. But in both cases the essence of the influence remains the same. Up to this point St. Bernardine follows strictly the previous teaching of, for instance, Peter Aureoli and Peter of Aquila.

But is it not repugnant that God should have willed Christ as passible *in primo signo*? Not at all, the Saint counters. Over and above the expiatory-satisfactory sense, Christ's Passion and death have a deeper and more essential meaning, a considerably wider range:

> The most perfect meriting (proper to the most perfect Mediator) requires actions concerning most difficult things and to suffer for the love of Him before whom he wishes to merit. For this reason it was necessary [*oportuit*] that Christ die because death realizes the fulness of His love for the Father and for His brethren.[22]

A rather daring thought indeed, and yet very true. The primary value of Christ's Passion and death is the manifestation of His boundless love toward His eternal Father and toward creatures. Even prescinding from sin, Christ was willed passible and mortal so that He could prove His love in the most unequivocal manner. This perspective finds its justification in the well-known Gospel passage: "There is no greater love than this: to lay down one's life for one's friends" (John 15:13).

The expiation-reparation aspect of Christ's redemptive role is, of course, an undeniable reality; but it is virtually contained in the factor of *love* which is at the very root of the entire design.[23] In this fashion St. Bernardine surmounts all the objections against a passible Incarnation. He not only does not endorse the famous distinction between passible and impassible Incarnation; he shows its incompatibility with Christ's primacy. At the same time, he rejects the second basis of that distinction by pointing out that passibility and death are not "evils," but the highest manifestation of divine love. Besides, if they were "evil," the Word could not have assumed them even *post praevisum lapsum.*

Thus the authentic doctrine of Christ's primacy, as understood by Scotus, Peter Aureoli, Peter of Aquila, St. Bernardine of Siena, and later by St. Francis de Sales,[24] did not disappear from the theological scene. There were always theologians who professed it, although admittedly, they constituted a minority. Among these, two distinguished scholars are particularly deserving of mention: St. Lawrence Brindisi (d. 1619) and Matthias Joseph Scheeben (d. 1888).

4. The Christocentrism of St. Lawrence of Brindisi

Using the concrete salvific plan willed by God as a point of departure, St. Lawrence spells out the fundamental consequences of the universal primacy of Christ.[25] The Savior was eternally willed by God as the supreme communication of His goodness; He was predestined as Head of the Mystical Body independently of every other creature, so that He might be the source, the center, and the end of all things. He is the exemplary, meritorious and final cause of every created reality.[26] Hence, both the natural and the supernatural orders depend on Christ as the first of the predestined. Human nature itself finds its exemplary cause in the God-Man.[27]

Christ's predestination refers simultaneously to the substance and to the modality in which it was actually realized. Christ was willed as a foundation in such a way that if the edifice to be built upon Him should ever need repairs, the reparation could be carried out on the same foundation without any change in the divine blueprint.[28]

Christ is the source of the essential grace and glory bestowed on angels and men. The mystery of the Incarnation was revealed to the angels, and it was this mystery that constituted the "test" and also the "way" through which the faithful angels arrived at eternal life.

Human freedom, as nature and as raised to grace, is the greatest resemblance to God and to Christ. It renders man capable of loving and, as such, it reflects the Love of God which is at the basis of everything. But it is at the same time a Christological love. Since Christ is the Supreme Lover outside of God, every other love is but a participation in the love of Christ.[29]

Not only was Christ predestined independently of the Fall; the Fall itself was permitted by God for the purpose of glorifying Christ: "I think that God permitted man's sin for the greater glory of Christ, in order to glorify Christ all the more."[30]

God accomplishes His design even by means of the sinful will of His creatures. And what is that design, specifically? The inexorable realization of the universal primacy of Christ, His glory from every viewpoint. Sin becomes the object of Christ's mercy through the redemptive role. That is why sin was permitted: in order to manifest the glory of Christ; just as several illnesses mentioned in the Gospel were permitted in order to reveal the divine healing power of the Messiah.[31]

In any case, nowhere does St. Lawrence refer to the distinction between an impassible Incarnation *ante praevisum lapsum*, and a passible Incarnation *post praevisum lapsum*. In this our holy Capuchin Doctor shows himself to be most faithful to the integral doctrine of the Savior's absolute and universal primacy without deviations or compromises.

5. The Scheeben Renewal

The authentic doctrine of Christ's universal primacy was propounded in a profound and often original manner by the outstanding German theologian, Matthias Joseph Scheeben (d. 1888).[32] The characteristic features of his theology are an attentive and controlled meditation on Sacred Scripture and a careful study of the Greek Fathers, especially St. Irenaeus, St. Athanasius, St. Cyril of Alexandria, and St. Gregory of Nyssa. From this point of view, he offers us the most complete treatment of the thesis. For this reason he may be rightly regarded as an important pioneer. His general conclusion is that the doctrine of the universal primacy of Christ, willed by God independently of creatures and especially of sin, is the only one that is fully warranted by Revelation.

According to our author, the very first decree of God, which is rooted in the communication of divine love, has for its object the Word Incarnate-Redeemer. Not a trace here of the distinction between passible and impassible Christ with reference to Adam's fall. For Scheeben, an Incarnation decreed by God exclusively or even primarily for our redemption, *post praevisum lapsum*, is a theological enormity which is incompatible with the very concept of God.

The author concentrates his attention particularly on the death of the Savior. He wishes to "liberate" our soteriology from all anthropocentrism and hamartiocentrism. The Incarnation is not *per se* a "'humiliation" on the part of God: "God stoops down to man's level by becoming man, without however quitting His exalted position; this condescension is precisely the truest and most perfect proof of His greatness."[33]

God lowered Himself *freely*, not compelled or conditioned by anything outside Himself. But does not St. Paul say that, by becoming man, the Son of God "emptied" Himself (Phil. 2:6-7) and hence underwent a "humiliation"? Certainly, Scheeben answers, but not because he became man, but because He assumed a passible, mortal nature when He had a right to a human nature that was glorious inasmuch as assumed by the Word.[34]

And here the famous distinction comes up again. If the Incarnation was willed by God independently of any creature, and if it is not *per se* a humiliation (since the Son of God would have a right to a glorious human nature), can it then be said that the "emptying" of Himself, or the taking of a passible nature was caused by the need to repair man's sin in a perfect manner and according to the demands of justice? If so, was not the "modality" of the Incarnation willed "after" the prevision of sin and because of it?

Not at all, Scheeben replies. It cannot be held that the "modality" of the Incarnation was determined by the Fall of man and by the need to repair it *de condigno*. The very same reasons which forbid us to teach that Christ was willed essentially for man, forbid us to teach that His passibility was essentially willed for the sake of man's sin.[35]

The current misunderstanding on this point stems from the idea that suffering is humiliating and that dying is a punishment. One can almost perceive a subtle leaning toward Monophysitism in so many theologians:

> . . . suffering and death are not in themselves ignominious; they are
> such only when they freight the subject with a compelling necessity,
> in consequence of nature or of sin, and against his will.[36]

Now, this is certainly not the case with Christ. The reason for His suffering and death are quite different. To begin with, passibility and death were not imposed on Him, but were freely assumed. And, as Scheeben remarks, in this case suffering may well be Christ's *supreme honor and glory*. Just what is the meaning, the purpose of suffering? Admittedly, on the purely natural level, one cannot but prefer joy to suffering. However, in relation to higher values, suffering and even death can be preferable to, and more glorious than joy and pleasure.

We take suffering upon ourselves only to gain a greater good. But a person suffers for others not only to relieve a need or to acquire a good for them, but also for the sole reason that he shows his love and esteem better by suffering than by all the deeds he performs for their benefit. . . . Suffering thus undertaken is obviously an act of the purest self-sacrifice and the most sublime virtue, and hence is more honorable and lovable than impassibility.[37]

And again Scheeben underlines:

. . . suffering is the more honorable the greater the freedom of the person concerned, and the less he is limited in his love to the bare need of the beloved. Hence we should be disparaging Christ's honor if we were to hold that He had allowed Himself to be subjected to suffering merely because, in consequence of sin, God had some need of the restitution of His honor, or the sinner had need of redemption.[38]

Christ appears most majestic in His sufferings precisely when we recall that He suffered "to give to God the highest possible glory, and to creatures the proof of a love which is worth incalculably more than the aid He accords them in their wretchedness.[39]

Scheeben observes daringly that the reason why the Word chose to assume a human nature rather than an angelic one, was precisely because the former made it possible for Him to die and thus show His love for the Father. The greatest glory of God and of Christ is the Cross, but it is not the need of the Cross that justifies the death of Christ. It is the other way around. "We believe rather that God has connected the restoration of the world with the Cross of His Son in order to glorify the Cross.[40] According to Scheeben, the profound reason for Christ's passibility and death is contained in the idea of *sacrifice* as the supreme manifestation of worship and love toward the Father. Since Jesus is God's greatest Lover, He freely assumed a passible body so as to be able to *immolate* Himself, dying on the Cross. Sacrifice is the most perfect and effective way to glorify God. "Therefore, if the God-Man is to promote the infinite glorification of God in the most effective and perfect manner possible, He must offer to God a latreutic sacrifice of infinite value."[41]

The redemption, then, is implicit in Christ's sacrifice which is essentially an act of love. *The Cross, however, in no way depends on the Fall.* Like the Incarnation, the death on the Cross is willed "before" the prevision of the Fall. And in the death on the Cross, as a response of love, is present every virtuality, such as reparation and expiation.

As we can see, in Scheeben's theology the primacy of Christ appears in its greatest extension and worth; it affects both the natural and the supernatural orders; it gives the keynote to the whole breadth of theology: nature and grace, predestination and salvation, knowledge of God and of the Blessed Trinity, the supernatural world, Mariology—literally everything is stamped with a Christological character. For our author, the whole of theology is rooted in Christology.

As far as the doctrine of the primacy is concerned, we should underline Scheeben's unitary and organic perspective, and the altogether original solution in connection with the death on the Cross. No trace here of either anthropocentrism or hamartiocentrism. We may note that the theological progress achieved in this connection especially by St. Bernadine, St. Lawrence and Scheeben is, in the last analysis, an authentic explicitation of Scotus' famous text:

> God first loves Himself; secondly, He loves Himself for others, and this is an ordered love; thirdly, He wishes to be loved by the One who can love Him in the highest way—speaking of the love of someone who is extrinsic to Him; and fourthly, He foresees the union of that nature which must love Him with the greatest love even if no one had fallen.[42]

Scotus, we may recall, had already brought out the fact that Christ's Passion and death must be evaluated within the dimension of love and freedom.[43]

Something which Scheeben, like St. Bernardine, does not explain fully is the notion of redemption, although for him also "to redeem" means considerably more than "to liberate from sin." The idea of "divinization" which he owes to the Greek Fathers and which constitutes the primary effect of Christ's primacy in relation to angels and men, already denotes an improvement over the views prevalent among Western theologians. In this broader perspective the primary sense of the Incarnation is an *elevating* function, namely, to introduce the creature into the Trinitarian life. The *liberating* facet connected with sin is a totally subordinate one.[44]

6. A Non-Catholic Voice: K. Barth

Among the modern authors who have vigorously insisted on the primacy of Christ, seeing it in all its vast dimension, Professor Karl Barth (d. 1968) unquestionably deserves to be mentioned. He does not follow, at least explicitly and directly, the current of Catholic theologians concernig this doctrine. His inspiration is different, eminently biblical and colored by Protestant motives. And yet, on central points, he arrives at conclusions which substantially coincide with the one we have been upholding. In fact. Barth's Christocentrism is of such amplitude that it excels all his other doctrines in importance. Guided by Sacred Scripture, he has truly exploited all the virtualities implied in the doctrine of the primacy. His exquisitely biblical methodology cannot but enrich the elucidations of Catholic theologians who maintain a rather speculative approach. Here we will limit ourselves to a brief reference to his thought. His treatment is, admittedly, difficult to synthesize.[45]

The very heart of Barth's extensive *Kirchliche Dogmatik*, the keystone of his theological thought is found in the notion of predestination—not in a generic sense, but inasmuch as it is realized in Christ.[46] In harmony with this, Barth believes that every part of dogmatic theology must be Christological. Christ's election constitutes the central point of all Christian mysteries. This is developed especially in the second volume of his *Dogmatik*.[47]

The author begins by rejecting the theories of predestination adopted in theology for centuries. First is the Augustinian and Calvinist idea that bases predestination on God's mercy.[48] Second, the idea of St. Bonaventure, St. Thomas and many Protestants who base it on divine omnipotence.[49] But these notions are not biblical and hence not acceptable. Sacred Scripture tells us that predestination is identical with the free divine decree of the Covenant. It is the divine decision by means of which God *in Christ* bends over toward man and makes a pact of friendship so as to introduce him into the divine life. Predestination is, then, a free, gratuitous gift, a grace, an act of *divine love*. It is the center of the Gospel, the totality of the Good News.[50] That means that predestination coincides with the divine act which freely wills Christ, since, according to Scripture, Christ is the center, the reason, the source of the Covenant. Actually, it is *in Christ* that God has made known His plan and brought it to completion. Predestination, then, does not result from God's absolute attributes; it is an act of His free will. In this respect, Barth's coincidence with Scotus is evident. Again, it is *in Christ* that God predestined everyone, and hence all predestination is essentially Christological, as St. Paul clearly teaches in his Epistle to the Ephesians (1:4-5). Sacred Scripture simply does not know of any other predestination.[51] It follows from all this that Christ was the *first* of the predestined, and this absolute primacy of His is attested to not only by St. Paul in Col. 1:15, but by the prologue of St. John's Gospel as well.[52]

In the free decree of predestination, when God decides to communicate

Himself *ad exra*,

> there is already present and presumed . . . the existence of the man whom He intends and loves from the very first, and in whom He intends and loves all other men. . . . In this free act of election of grace the Son of the Father is no longer just the eternal Logos . . . but He is also the very God and the very Man He will become in time. In the divine act of predestination there pre-exists the Jesus Christ who as the Son of the eternal Father and the child of the Virgin Mary, will become and be the Mediator of the covenant between God and man. . . . He is (the covenant's) eternal basis.[53]

We have quoted this text to show that, for Barth, Christ's predestination *in ordine intentionis* and His absolute primacy are revealed and affirmed in the very order of execution. Hence, we are not dealing here with a mere theological opinion, but with the very substance of biblical Revelation. It is interesting to note the perfect, almost verbal agreement with Scotus when Barth describes God's movement toward His creatures.[54]

Barth also examines at length the seventeenth century controversy among Protestants between the "supralapsarii" and the "infralapsarii"—a debate that has its parallel in the well-known Catholic polemic between Thomists and Scotists. The question was asked whether the plan of predestination concerned man "creabilis et labilis" or rather man as "creatus et lapsus"; whether the decree of predestination was prior or subsequent to the prevision of the Fall. For Barth both sides are wrong inasmuch as both admitted that the object of predestination was the individual, directly, and that it was based on an absolute decree distinct from Christ. However, between the two positions, the less erroneous was the "supralapsaria" because it situated predestination before the prevision of sin. The substance of this solution is correct, but it must be viewed form the perspective of Christ's absolute primacy in the order of predestination.[55] Thus Barth substantially propounds the Scotistic thesis, even though in a new and autonomous fashion, as the very synthesis and marrow of Revelation, as the direct result of his attentive study of Sacred Scripture and without taking into account the Catholic theological tradition.

Another aspect of the Covenant studied by Barth is its relationship to sin and redemption. Owing to Adam's sin, the Covenant assumes, historically, the form of reconciliation. However, the occurrence of sin, for all its gravity, has neither destroyed nor modified the initial Covenant. The Covenant is not merely a "reaction" to the Fall; it is in no way conditioned by it. The Covenant carries out what God had planned from the beginning, gratuitously and unconditionally, in Christ Jesus. The divine plan of the Covenant, therefore, is what constitutes the permanent and immutable basis of the reconciliation.[56]

Going even deeper into this matter, our author examines the relationship between the covenant and creation. He does so according to his understanding of Christ's primacy. From this perspective, the Covenant would seem to require the existence of the world and of man; it is their end. With this as a basis, Barth undertakes a very lengthy development of the nature of cosmology, and the theological dimension of the universe.[57]

Anthropology is an essential part of theological cosmology. In this, too, Christ's primacy is the key to solve all problems. Since Christ and the Covenant are the end governing creation, it follows that, for Barth, God's primitive intention with regard to man is broader than the mere decision to create. That is to say, the order of nature is immersed in a much vaster and higher framework, namely, that of the supernatural Covenant *in Christo Jesu*.

According to Barth, when God created, He willed not only man's existence, but his salvation as well. Salvation, however, is not something demanded by man. It is a free gift of God. Since the divine intention of the Covenant dominates the created order and constitutes its end, we are justified in concluding that such intention "precedes" creation; it is "prior" according to the order of predestination. Hence, man's destination to the Covenant in Christ Jesus is the reason and the foundation of God's creative will.[58]

Here, too, we can easily rediscover Scotus' viewpoint based on the hierarchy of beings and of values, according to the celebrated axiom: "Ordinate volens prius videtur velle hoc quod est fini propinquius, etc. , "[59] except that Barth always establishes his conclusion, not by means of direct theological reasoning, but rather by recourse to Scripture.

But the author also develops the doctrine of the primacy with rigorous reasoning and with a breadth of vision that is unique in the history of theology. In fact, both Barth and Scotus use the same pivotal premise for their demonstration, namely: from the order of execution, in which Sacred Scripture portrays Christ as the center and the scope of all divine works *ad extra* in the natural and supernatural orders, they rise to the order of intention to conclude that Christ's predestination is truly the very heart and substance of the divine design which embraces nature and grace. And it is likewise worth noting that, for Barth even as for Scotus, the notion of predestination (while not exactly the same in both) is precisely the clue to a correct understanding of Christ's primacy and its wide implications.[60]

To sum up: Absolutely speaking, Karl Barth was not a pioneer in this matter of expounding the doctrine of Christ's primacy. The novelty for which we are indebted to him lies particuarly in his methodology, namely, in his having established the primacy on the basis of biblical exegesis rather than on the exploitation of theological deductions. On this point, the great theological opus of this Protestant scholar constitutes a really remarkable contribution, a precious enrichment which ought to be taken into account by our own Catholic students of this doctrine.

6.
The Paduan Scotistic Theologians

Theological Schools trace their genesis back to the Middle Ages. In the post-Tridentine period they took on more rigid and definitive characteristics. Theologians adhered to a precise tradition in such a way that it suffices to know what School they were associated with to establish at once their basic tenets. Theological activity, lacking for the most part creative genius, assumed an ever more uniform character within the lines of the various Schools. Nevertheless, one can point to certain peculiarities of post-Tridentine theology which were found in every theological School, peculiarities which differentiate it notably from classic Scholasticism and also from the more recent era. We have in mind a marked intellectualism that exploits all the resources of philosophy, especially logic and Aristotelian metaphysics, as a method of theological exposition; again, the excessively long treatment given to a subject; the undue importance attached to marginal questions; the polemical tone used against the adversary; the useless subtleties which often make one lose sight of the vital values of theology; and finally, the frequently superstitious loyalty to every position defended by one's own School, a loyalty that can only stifle creativity and legitimate development. And yet, side by side with the above shortcomings, it is only fair to note some positive factors such as the vigor and enthusiasm with which theological problems are treated, and the incisiveness of thought and expression so generally observable. The numerous and sturdy in-folios of post-Tridentine theology constitute an inexhaustible and imperishable mine of theological knowledge.

In this chapter we wish to limit our investigation to the seventeenth century, which was undoubtedly the Golden Age of Scotism. and within this time-limit we will mention only those who taught at the friary of St. Anthony of Padua (widely known as "Convento del Santo") and at the theological faculty of Padua University. We must point out at the outset that these theologians are not particularly original; they move within the limitations of the School and are a faithful mirror thereof. The subject matter is identical in all of them; the framing of the problem varies little; the argumentation is substantially the same. Nevertheless, they display a certain amount of sharpness in their reasoning, and also extensive erudition.[1] Three of them in particular will now occupy our attention: Fabbri, Belluti, and Mastri.

1. Philip Fabbri, O.F.M. Conv. (d. 1630)

Philip Fabbri (Latinized as "Faber"), professor at the theological faculty of Padua University during several decades, has left us, among other works, a voluminous course of theology: *Disputationes Theologicae in quattuor libros Sententiarum*. The first edition appeared in Venice, 1613; the second, revised and corrected by the author himself, was published in Venice, 1619 in three large volumes in-folio. He treats the question of Christ's primacy in the *Disputationes in tertium librum Sententiarum*, following the classic division of Peter Lombard.[2] Unlike most of the theologians of the period, he discusses our topic in the context of Christ's predestination, and not in connection with the Savior's merits and satisfactions. This is worth noting because it shows how the author radically eliminates hamartiocentrism from his perspective.

Our author begins by stressing that predestination, in general, is an entirely gratuitous gift on God's part; that it is in no way conditioned by the creature because it takes place "ante praevisa merita." This, the author points out correctly, is a teaching common to most theologians, and especially St. Bonaventure and St. Thomas.[3]

Fabbri then approaches the problem of whether Christ's predestination was absolute or conditioned by the Fall. On this point, which is "grave and much disputed," the author says there are two positions.[4] He discusses both extensively, with clarity and objectivity.

One preliminary observation made by Fabbri seems to us worth bearing in mind. Scotus, he writes, proposes his opinion "multis rationibus, protestatur tamen hoc asserere absque praejudicio; Scotus enim praecipue inter Scholasticos semper *maxima modestia* utitur."[5] This should be remembered by those who claim that the Subtle Doctor was a proud man bent on demolishing the teaching of other theologians in order to promote his own eccentric views. Of all medieval theologians, Scotus stands out as perhaps the most serene and objective, always extremely humble in proposing his own ideas. Unfortunately, this very modesty (which he often expresses by a "mihi videtur") had deceived not a few superficial readers.

Thus, for instance, in connection with the Doctor's teaching on our Blessed Lady's Immaculate Conception, some have said that he had not actually made up his mind, that he was expressing only an opinion. Evidently, these critics do not take into consideration Scotus' characteristic manner of expression. As with Scotus, so also with Fabbri, the most important efficacious argument in favor of Christ's absolute primacy is taken from the very notion of predestination. If everyone else's predestination is *ante praevisum lapsum*, then, *a fortiori*, the predestination of Christ, the Head of all the predestined, must have been absolute, independent of any created factor such as Adam's disobedience. St. Thomas himself, as noted previously, affirms that predestination does not presuppose any condition on the part of creatures.[6]

Fabbri then proceeds to refute Cajetan's main objection to the effect that the three distinct orders of nature, grace, and hypostatic union are willed by God in a successive order. Our author answers that in Cajetan's objection there is an illegitimate passage from the order of execution to that of intention. Besides, if sin belongs to the order of nature and Christ is willed only as its rememdy, it follows that the predestination of Christ depends on something temporal and creaturely, against the general principle held by all, including the Angelic Doctor. Again, if the position of Cajetan were correct, then the sin of those who crucified Christ would have been foreseen before Christ Himself was. Many other arguments are advanced in this connection.[7]

A second basic argument which Fabbri borrows from Scotus is the famous axiom: "Ordinate volens prius videtur velle id quod est fini propinquius, etc." Since Christ is the one nearest the end and is, in fact, the irreplaceable way which leads all to the end (John 14:6), He must have been willed by God before all the rest. It is useless for Cajetan to answer that the axiom is valid *de possibili* but not *de facto*, since God, being free, *can* will that which is a greater good for the sake of a lesser one. Fabbri's rejoinder is terse and to the point:

> Verum haec responsio [Cajetani] non satisfacit argumento. Propositio enim ista [Scotus' axiom] secumfert suam probationem: dicit enim: *Ordinate* volens, non: *absolute* volens. Quandocumque ergo est agens liberum et vult libere aliqua plura ordinate, idest, ut illa sunt volibilia et inter illa unum est magis volibile quam aliud, illa voluntas prius et magis vult illud quod *in se* est magis et prius volibile quam illud quod *in se* est minus volibile. Alioquin non esset ordinata voluntas, sicut qui diligeret magis corpus quam animam non vellet ordinate. Propositio ergo illa major est vera simpliciter et de possibili et de facto

in voluntate ordinata.[8]

We are not dealing, then, with hypothetical choices, or *de possibili*. An objectively greater good is *de facto* willed more intensely than a lesser one. God cannot will the greater for the lesser because that would involve a contradiction and an absurdity. And why is that? Because it is God's will that creates the good existing ouside of Him. He does not "find" an object lovable (volibile); He creates that lovableness by the very fact that He wills it. That is why it is irrational to say that God can will the greater for the lesser. It would be equivalent to saying that God loves the lesser more than the greater, and that, therefore, the lesser is more than the greater—a palpable contradiction.[9]

There remains a difficult point. Was Christ predestined *in primo signo* as Redeemer? As noted before, this is the weak aspect of the solution offered by so many Scotists. Fabbri acknowledges that Scotus himself was undecided on the question. The Subtle Doctor seems to teach, according to Fabbri, that Christ's coming *in carne passibili* was decreed only after the prevision of the Fall. As we have already observed, for Scotus, this duplication of decrees is doubtful. For Fabbri, as for so many others, it is certain.

But does not this duplication of decrees imply a change or modification in the divine plan, as the Thomists object? Our author answers: There is no change, because *in primo signo* God wills the Incarnation neither as passible nor as impassible, but only in its substance. But, the adversaries insist, how can we say that God wills something in the abstract, without its concrete modalities? Fabbri replies by making lengthy and subtle distinctions between the *scientia simplicis intelligentiae* and the *scientia visionis*. His answer, however, leaves us unconvinced. The question is not about possibilities but about the real.[10] We must acknowledge that the author fails to meet the Thomistic objection successfully. Nor—come to think of it— could he have done so, considering his idea of "redemption." With the theologians of the period, Fabbri believes that "to redeem" means exclusively "to liberate from sin." Hence, Christ could not have been foreseen as Redeemer "before" the prevision of sin.[11]

Surely the above perspective does not harmonize with the doctrine of the primacy of Christ as we have explained it. If we admit the theory of the two decrees, does it not follow that the death of Christ, the greatest and most sublime act of His life of love, was "caused" by sin? Fabbri affirms this explicitly.[12] But isn't that incompatible with the *absolute* character of Christ's primacy?

Finally, since Christ merited the redemption with His death, how can He be the source of the angels' grace? Were they not glorified "before" the prevision of sin? On this point, Fabbri is consistent. He denies that Christ merited the essential grace of the angels. The angels were not redeemed by Christ even *praeservative*, like Mary.[13] Again we point out: If this be so, then Christ's primacy is no longer absolute and universal. Jesus is no longer the "firstborn of *every* creature," as St. Paul clearly proclaims (Col. 1:15).

2. Bonaventure Belluti, O.F.M.Conv. (d. 1676)

The theology of Bonaventure Belluti concerning the Incarnation is found in a monograph entitled *Disputationes de Incarnatione Dominica ad mentem Doctoris Subtilis* (Cataniae, 1645). It embodies the lectures he had imparted to his Padua students during so many years of teaching. The question of the primacy is treated in the section devoted to the final causality of the Incarnation, although some aspects of it are touched elsewhere.

Having explained the "status quaestionis,"[14] Belluti introduces us to three opinions on the subject: the Thomist, the Scotist, and the "Tertia via." Strangely enough, Suárez appears in the second group (although with reservations); the third group includes Raphael Aversa, Cler. Reg. Min. (d. 1657) and Gaspar Hurtado, S.J. (d. 1647).[15]

In his defense of the Scotistic thesis, Belluti concentrates his greatest efforts, not on theological reasoning, but rather on the biblical and patristic foundations. Among the biblical passages he examines are Eccl. 24:5; Prov. 8:22; Col. 1:15-20; Rom. 8:29-30; 1 Cor. 15:49; and Phil. 3:21. As to the Fathers, he quotes a few texts from St. Augustine and St. Cyril, and then St. Anselm. The author completely ignores the vast corpus of Greek Fathers on our subject. The theological argument is reduced to a few lines devoted to the notion of predestination and the hierarchy of beings.[16] Much lengthier, however, is his handling of the objections raised against Scotus (e.g., those of Cajetan, Aversa, Hurtado), although he contributes nothing new to the question.

Concerning the distinction between the substance and the modality of the Incarnation, our author accepts it as being beyond question; it follows logically from his limited understanding of redemption. Thus he states that "ante praevisionem peccati Christus non fuit electus redemptor."[17] Belluti is so convinced that Suárez is a Scotist that he goes so far as to endorse his theory of the two total motives of the Incarnation.[18] As if on second thought, however, he confesses that, unless we admit the subordination of one motive to the other the Suarezian theory is philosophically untenable.

Even more untenable is the reasoning of the Doctor Eximius on the "optimus modus" chosen by God to will the Incarnation. This, according to Belluti, leads to subordinating the Incarnation to the sin of man.[19] Another question discussed by Belluti is whether Christ's predestination was the cause of ours.[20] He duly distinguishes the various aspects under which the matter may be considered: exemplary cause, final cause, and efficient-meritorious cause.[21] Against Vázquez, our author maintains that Christ was the "verum exemplar ad instar cujus Deus coeteros praedestinavit electos." Sacred Scripture, especially St. Paul's Epistle to the Colossians, openly teaches this; and among the Fathers, St. Augustine is categorical on the subject.[22] The thesis is grounded on the fact that Christ is the Head of all the predestined and that they must therefore be conformed to His grace (cf. Rom. 8:29). But grace is nothing but a share in the quality of Son which is proper to Christ. *Ergo.*[23]

Again, Sacred Scripture clearly teaches that Christ, not only as God (as Vázquez claims) but even as the *incarnate* Word, is the final cause of all creatures. The Epistle to the Colossians is unequivocal on the matter.

Concerning Christ's efficient-meritorious causality, Belluti mentions Suárez's opinion that Christ merited the election of all to eternal life,[24] but adds: "Dico tamen Christum non meruisse nobis praedestinationem et electionem primam ad gloriam, etiam in ratione dilectionis."[25] The reason is that merit, formally speaking, is related to the reward as to its proper end. Hence merit always presupposes the end. Now, eternal life is precisely the end presupposed by the merit of Christ and thus it is not merited but freely and gratuitously donated by God.[26]

The second problem has to do with the sanctifying grace of the angels and of Adam *in statu innocentiae*. Can we say that Christ merited that grace? Many deny it, but "affirmativa pars est probabilior"; it is logical for those who hold that Christ's predestination was independent of the Fall.[27]

At this juncture a very serious question arises. Sacred Scripture never states that Christ came for the angels. Besides, Christ's merit was consummated through His death, and one cannot say that Christ died for the angels. Finally, it would follow that Christ was the Redeemer of the angels and of innocent Adam who had no sin to be liberated from.[28]

Belluti states his position thus: It is true that the Bible and the Fathers frequently present the Incarnation under the aspect of "liberation from sin." But this is because they have in mind the case of the human race which is historically and *de facto* under the domination of sin. Nevertheless, when Sacred Scripture speaks of sanctification, blessings, gratification and the like, it either includes the angels or does not exlude them. The same holds for the merits flowing from Christ's death. They often refer to "liberation from sin," but they cannot be reduced to that. Does not Sacred Scripture clearly affirm that the Savior merited for Himself too (Phil. 2:7-11)? The same way Christ merited His own glorification by means of His death without this involving any "liberation from sin." He also merited the angels' glorification even though they had no sin.[29]

The author goes even further. Christ, he says, can be called the Redeemer of the angels, not in the proper sense of freeing them from the captivity of sin, but in a broad sense "quia praeservavit non a peccato quod debuissent necessario incurrere, sed a peccato quod *poterant* incurrere pro sua libertate."[30] The observation is worth noting, for it is a felicitous and genial application of the doctrine of Christ's primacy against the widespread belief that redemption was equivalent to liberating from sin. For Belluti, on the contrary, to redeem (at least in the broad sense) is fundamentally equivalent to raising someone to the supernatural state. This is the basic concept of redemption. It may be implemented either by liberating a finite freedom from the fallibility which is connatural to it precisely as finite, or by liberating it from a fall already incurred. But the two modalities are accidental and do not change the essence of the liberation.

Summing up, we must admit that, unfortunately, not everything in Belluti's treatise is deserving of praise. We have already recalled the meagerness of his theological arguments in favor of the primacy; then again, his thought is at times unclear, superficial and not very logical. On the positive side, however, we must call attention to his effort to give the primacy a more biblical and patristic foundation; to his excellent handling of the threefold causality of Christ; and to his penetrating insight relative to the meaning of the Savior's death, and the application to the angels of the redemption *via praeservationis*. This is, as we all know, the genial idea which the Marian Doctor had introduced in connection with Mary's Immaculate Conception, and which is now borrowed by Belluti, as he himself acknowledges.[31]

3. Bartholomew Mastri, O.F.M.Conv. (d. 1673)

Bartholomew Mastri (Latinized: *Mastrius*) was born in Meldola in 1602 and devoted his whole life to serious study. He is generally regarded as the "prince" of post-Tridentine Scotists—a title he abundantly deserves on account of his voluminous publications in the fields of philosophy and theology.[32] His merit lies, not only in his faithful adherence to Scotus' thought, but also in the breadth of his information, the amplitude of his horizon, the solidity and even elegance of his presentation. He was, in a word, a thoroughly skilled theologian.

The third volume of his copious *Commentary on the Four Books of Sentences* is devoted, for the most part, to Christology.[33] Of the seven lengthy "Disputationes" making up the third volume, five deal with Christology, covering some four hundred pages in-folio.

The first three "disputationes" discuss the possibility of the Incarnation, the nature of the hypostatic union, Christ's grace, sanctity, merits. The theme of Christ's primacy is inserted into the fourth "Disputatio" which bears the general title: *De satisfactione Christi Domini.* The fifth "Disputatio" examines the problem of Christ's intellect and will.

The very fact that the author includes the primacy of Christ in his discussion of the Savior's redemptive satisfaction, already suggests that he has been influenced by the hamartiocentrism of his time. Fortunately, he manages to surmount the narrow perspective so common to his contemporaries.

Introducing the problem, Mastri acknowledges that "haec est celeberrima controversia inter omnes ad tertiam partem vel tertium librum Sententiarum spectantes."[34] He then indicates the three solutions advanced: the Thomist, the Scotist, and the third, proposed by Suárez, Hurtado, Granado, and Aversa.[35] The problem centers, as the author repeatedly insists, not on a "possible" Incarnation, but on the only Incarnation which was actually and *de facto* willed by God.

According to Mastri, the primary end or purpose of the Incarnation was not our redemption from sin, but the intrinsic excellence of the mystery itself and the manifestation of the goodness and other attributes of God.[36]

Three main arguments are advanced in favor of the thesis. The most compelling is, of course, that based on the very nature of predestination. Mastri studies it from every angle. He turns first to Sacred Scripture, particularly the passages of Prov. 8:22; Eph. 1:4, Rom. 8:29; 1 Cor. 3:21-23; Col. 1:15ff. From these texts, the author observes, it emerges clearly that Christ is the Head of all the predestined and, therefore, willed before all others.[37] Some, it is true, have endeavored to invalidate this argument by claiming that the biblical title "firstborn" applies to Christ as God, not as Man. But this interpretation, the author stresses, openly clashes with the context and with the interpretation proposed by the Fathers.

Two other objections are generally raised by the Thomists in this connection. First, some say that Sacred Scripture teaches the primacy of Christ's predestination *in ordine excellentiae et dignitatis,* but not *in ordine efficientiae* with regard to others. Mastri retorts: This restriction is manifestly groundless since excellence and dignity rest on an ontological reality which constitutes the primary object of divine predestination. Besides, Sacred Scripture teaches not only Christ's exemplary, final and meritorious causality as regards all creatures, but His universal efficient causality as well. This is directly attested to by St. Paul in his Epistle to the Colossians: "In him [Christ] everything in heaven and on earth was created. All were created through him and for him. He is before all else that is. In him everything continues in being" (1:16-17).

The second difficulty is to the effect that, just as God's desire (*voluntate antecedenti*) that all men be saved does not mean that all men are *de facto* saved, so it may be said that God willed the Incarnation *voluntate antecedenti*, without concluding that He willed it efficaciously and *de facto* independent of the Fall. This, however, in Mastri's judgment, is nothing but a subterfuge, because the Bible always speaks of an efficacious will on the part of God; it describes the concrete and precise design of salvation as achieved by Christ; it does not deal with mere possibles.

The primary theological argument, as already noted, always remains the one based on the very nature of predestination, and it is handled by our author with great competence. He remind us that it is *doctrina communis*, accepted also by St. Thomas and his followers, that the predestination of creatures to glory (and hence to grace) is totally free and gratuitous on God's part; unlike the case of reprobation, it presupposes nothing on the part of creatures. If this holds for all, then *a fortiori* it holds for Christ, who is the first and greatest of all the predestined. That is why His predestination, as exemplar of all others, cannot depend on the sin of other men, "alioquin filius naturalis esset delectus propter servos et dependenter ab amore servorum."[38]

This argument based on the nature of predestination is so cogent that the Thomists have not been able to answer it, except by having recourse to Cajetan's well-known (and generally abandoned) theory of the three successive orders. Mastri observes that the above reasoning leads nowhere because it is based on Cajetan's awkward confusion of the order of execution with that of intention "qui tamen sunt valde diversi, adeo ut quod prius est in uno est posterius in alio."[39] If Cajetan's theory were correct, several absurdities would follow, such as, as we have seen, the fact that the sin of those who crucified Christ would have been foreseen before the Savior Himself had been foreseen.

The second theological argument is that of the *ordinate volens* based on the objective hierarchy of values, in virtue of which the lesser cannot be the end, purpose and scope of the greater. Arguing from this premise, Mastri shows that Christ could not have been willed for the sake of creatures; it was the other way around. The Incarnation, then, could not have depended on any creaturely factor, least of all the sin of man.

In order to elude the efficacy of the argument, the Thomists have recourse to the distinction between "final cause" and "material cause." Christ, they claim, was willed first from the viewpoint of final causality, but *in genere causae materialis*, He was willed "after" the prevision of Adam's sin. Our author, borrowing an observation made by Rada,[40] wonders how sin can be regarded as a material cause in this connection. According to the Thomists themselves, sin is the "occasion," the "condition," the motive" etc. of the Incarnation. If this is so, sin is what "moves" God (humanly speaking) to become man. Now, a factor that "moves" an agent to produce something belongs in the area of *final*, not material causality. Hence, the appeal to material causality here serves only to create confusion. The Thomists' answer to the "ordinate volens" argument is reduced to this: Christ was willed after the prevision of sin and as a remedy thereof. But He was also willed as the end of all creatures. So, He *became* the end of a world which had *already* been created and *already* raised to the supernatural order. The sophism involved is patent.

Another distinction appealed to by the Thomists is that between the "finis cui" and the "finis cujus gratia." Christ's glory, they say, is the "finis cujus gratia" God decreed the Incarnation, but our liberation from sin was the "finis cui." Mastri retorts: Either the above statement embodies the Scotistic opinion, or it constitutes a vicious circle. In other words, either the Incarnation is willed for its own sake (the Scotistic thesis), or it is originally willed as a means of liberating us from sin, in which case this latter is the "finis cujus gratia" and not the "finis cui." One cannot be end and means in the same genus of causality; it is a contradiction.[41]

The third theological argument is supplied by the absolute gratuity of the divine communcations. Here, too, Mastri depends on Scotus: "Primo Deus intellexit se sub ratione primi Boni. . . . In tertio, volens suae bonitatis manifestationem, etc."[42] Mercy, then, is not the ultimate explanation of God's actions, but rather His gratuitous goodness. God is never "occasioned" in His acting; He is sovereignly free. The noblest terminus of His greatest communication *ad extra* is Jesus Christ, the God-Man who can love and worship the Father in the most perfect manner. It is simply absurd to think that the most noble product of God's love and the most sublime response to that love owed its existence to the Fall of man.[43]

As we have indicated before, the relationship between the Incarnation and the Redemption has not been explained satisfactorily by the majority of Scotus' disciples. Mastri is no exception. His thesis is terse: "Christus non fuit primo praedestinatus ut Redemptor."[44] He places two decrees in God: one concerning the substance of the Incarnation, the second, its modality. The former precedes the prevision of Adam's Fall, while the latter presupposes it.

The first reason why this is so must be found in the fact that to redeem means exclusively to liberate from sin. The second reason is taken from the meaning and value of Christ's death. The Incarnation, Mastri states, differs from Christ's Passion and death in that "Incarnatio est propter se amabilis tamquam finis aliorum operum Dei; passio vero et mors Christi non propter se, sed in remedium peccati et ut medicina."[45]

Mastri is well aware of the grave difficulties against this solution. For example, how can anyone say that Christ's death has only a satisfactory value? If everything in this mystery is governed by love, how can the supreme action of Christ—His death on the Cross—be reduced and diminished to the mere category of punishment, expiation and satisfaction? How can anyone say that Christ's death, the supreme act of His love, is not "per se amabilis"? Would it not be more in harmony with Scotistic thinking to say, not that Christ was decreed passible on account of sin, but rather that sin was permitted by God for the sake of Christ "ut Christus haberet quod per suam passionem curaret"?[46]

To all this, Mastri replies monotonously: the death of Christ had only a penal-satisfactory value; hence it could not have been decreed "before" the prevision of the Fall.[47] This seems to be an absolute and irremovable point of departure.

But does not Sacred Scripture itself (Phil. 2:7-11) portray the Passion and death as having been willed by God for the *exaltation* of Christ? Certainly, our author answers, but this is only an accidental and extrinsic exaltation which is owed Him because He redeemed us.[48] Obviously, on this point, Mastri is heavily influenced by anthropocentrism and hamartiocentrism. He does not share the freedom and daring of his colleague Belluti.

There is another difficulty against the distinction between the substance and the modality of the Incarnation. The divine intellect does not reach its terminus in an abstract fashion but with all its concrete formalities. Nor does the efficacious will of God ever refer to things "in universali sed in particulari; alioqin actus ille non esset efficax."[49] It is impossible, then, to speak of the divine decree referring to the concrete order while abstracting from the Incarnation's possibility.

According to Mastri, some Scotists answer the above objection as follows: It is true that when God decrees something, He decides on all its circumstances; but this refers only to those circumstances which are intrinsic to the thing itself, not to those that are extrinsic, i.e., those that are separable from the former. Since passibility is extrinsic to the Incarnation, one can be decreed without the other.

Mastri finds the above answer unsatisfactory because, in his judgment, neither passibility nor impassibility can be considered as being "extrinsic" to human nature.[50] The author's own answer is formulated as follows: the initial decree of the Incarnation included God's desire for Christ's soul to enjoy the beatific vision. This beatific vision, *per se*, involved the extension of its influence to the body; that is to say, it contained *virtualiter* the impassibility of the body also. Nevertheless, this latter was not the explicit terminus of the divine decree. That is why God *in primo signo* did not decide whether Christ's body would be passible or impassible because neither possibility was intended directly, although as a consequence of the beatific vision the divine decree would have, *per se*, involved the body's impassibilty. In short, in virtue of the first decree, Christ was constituted impassible "tantum virtualiter et in causa, non autem formaliter et in se."[51] According to this, after the prevision of sin, God did not change His previous decree. He simply hindered the glory of Christ's soul from being extended to His body, so that the body actually preserved the passibility which is natural to the human composite.[52]

The above answer is, admittedly, subtle and suggestive. And yet, we find it unsatisfactory because it does not give the death of the Savior all the relevance it deserves; and what is worse, it makes it contingent on man's sin. The supreme act of the God-Man cannot be "conditioned" by evil.

A few decades before Mastri, the Jesuit Gabriel Vázquez (d. 1604) had condensed the Scotistic view into what he considered a dead-end dilemma. It went like this: If in the present economy Christ had come, *Adamo non peccante*, He would have come either passible or impassible. Not passible because, *ex hypothesi*, there would be no sin. Not impassible either, because God never decreed an impassible coming. If He had, then Christ certainly would have come impassible—which He did not. Or else God changed His plans on account of the Fall of man; but this is absurd. Vázquez concludes, *vi praesentis decreti*, Christ would not have come if Adam had not sinned.[53]

Mastri seeks to elude the above dilemma by repeating that the impassibility of Christ's body was willed *in primo signo* only virtually and not formally; hence there is no change in the divine decree. Besides, as other theologians have pointed out, Vázquez is actually using a paralogism. We can show its lack of foundation by applying it, for instance, to the case of Adam. Before the prevision of the Fall, God created Adam either mortal or immortal. He did not create him mortal because death is the consequence of sin. He did not create him immortal either because otherwise this divine decree was either not carried out or was changed on account of sin, which is absurd. Therefore, *vi praesentis decreti*, God created Adam neither mortal nor immortal. Therefore, just as we can say that God decreed to create Adam before the prevision of sin, but determined his mortality or immortality *contingent* on his disobedience or on his perseverance, the same thing happened in Christ's case. His passibility or impassibility *de facto* was *contingent* on man's sin, and this leaves the first decree untouched.[54] Here, too, Mastri displays the keenness of his mind, but does not succeed in surmounting the grave obstacle of making the death of Christ dependent on sin.

Over and above these difficulties, there remains to be examined the objection which all Thomists regard as basic: The Church, interpreting the date of Revelation, assures us that God willed the Incarnation "propter nos homines et propter nostram salutem."

Mastri replies that not even the Thomists themselves accept their own reasoning fully. For example, they admit that the Incarnation was not decreed as a remedy for sin "ut propter finem totalem nec principalius amatum; hunc enim finem dicunt esse ipsius Christi gloriam et exaltationem; ergo talis finis non erat sola redemptio."[55] One minute they tell us that the Incarnation was willed *only* for the sake of our redemption; then in the next breath they distinguish, they interpret, they turn the order around by saying, for example, that Christ is not *totally* for sin, etc. Now, if the Thomists do not take their own principle literally and rigorously, why do they expect others to do so? The fact is, Mastri continues, that Sacred Scripture nowhere states that Christ came "only and exclusively" on account of our sins. It suffices to recall the passages from St. Paul's Epistles to the Colossians and to the Ephesians to the contrary.

Turning next to the problem of the angels, it is well known that the theological explanation of the grace of the angels and of innocent Adam has a direct bearing on the doctrine of Christ's primacy. The reason for the nexus is obvious. Mastri discusses this topic, not in the *Disputatio quarta* where he treats of the primacy, but in the *Disputatio tertia* which is entitled: "De merito Christi Domini et aliorum per ipsum."

Our author asks whether Christ merited the first sanctifying grace of the angels and of our first parents before the Fall.[56] Note well that the problem is whether Christ *merited* the grace, not whether that grace *derived* from Him. Some affirm that Christ merited the grace of the angels. For the Scotists of this group, the reason is simple: Christ was predestined *ante praevisum peccatum* as Head of all creatures, and the grace of the angels and of innocent Adam certainly does not depend on the prevision of the Fall. Christ was capable of meriting by all the actions of His life even prescinding from His death.

Many other Scotists, however, deny that Christ merited the angels' grace because they see a necessary nexus between the Savior's merit and His passibility, and the latter, in their opinion, was willed only after the prevision of sin and as a remedy thereof.[57]

Where does Mastri himself stand on this question? His position is rather interesting. He begins by sharing the views of the second group, stating that Christ could not have merited the grace of the angels because His merit derives totally from His Passion and death which follow the prevision of sin.[58]

But is Christ not the Head of the angels? If so, does it not follow that they owe their grace to Him? Mastri seems somewhat perplexed. He acknowledges the weight of this argument, but cannot quite manage to bring it into harmony with his views on the nexus between Christ's merits and His death. Thus he settles for a compromise: In order for Christ to be the true Head of the angels, it is sufficient for Him to have merited for them an *accidental* influx of illumination, glory and happiness.[59] A truly disconcerting observation, considering everything he had written on Christ's primacy. Fortunately, that is not his last word on the subject. At the end of the lengthy discussion, he executes a complete about-face and openly joins the ranks of those who hold that the essential grace of the angels was indeed merited by Christ. He does this because this opinion "cedit in majorem Christi Domini excellentiam."[60] This is an application of the well-known "law" formulated by Scotus and now recalled by Mastri:

> In commendando enim Christum, malo excedere quam deficere a laude sibi debita, si propter ignorantiam oporteat in alterutrum incidere.[61]

4. Observations

Let us now give a brief overview. The first thing to be noted in the three authors we have examined is that they did not add anything original to what their predecessors had already contributed. There is nothing surprising about that, since it was not their intention to propose novel intuitions. Mastri himself makes an explicit declaration to that effect in the very preface to the third volume of his Commentary. Their task was to illustrate the Scotistic tradition as they knew it. That tradition was in itself original enough.

The second feature we would like to mention refers to the importance our authors attach to the Incarnation. For them, the mystery of the Incarnation with all its aspects always retained a striking centrality. The redemption was seen, as it were, within the framework of the Incarnation. They did not, of course, bring out the centrality of the Incarnation in relation to the other branches of the theological discipline. They hardly portrayed all theology as being Christological. Here the intuitions of a St. Bonaventure would have been a definitive asset. But the ambition of our authors was to be always faithful followers of Scotus, and they did not discover in their Master the limpid and decisive Christocentrism of the Seraphic Doctor as a universal theological perspective.

The third aspect of their theology is the importance given to the question of Christ's primacy and the independence of the Incarnation from the Fall of Adam. On this point they were all in perfect agreement. This is, as it were, a family heritage, like the doctrine of Mary's Immaculate Conception which they all championed decisively and with enthusiasm.

Our theologians developed the argument with a speculative method. Their manner of reasoning is eminently Scholastic. The positive approach is not absent, but it certainly does not receive the ample consideration we would have preferred. The culture and the tastes of the times had a lot to do with this.

It is only fair to note that our authors never succeeded in presenting adequately the relationship between the Incarnation and the redemptive role of the Savior. This was due, as we pointed out, to the influence of hamartiocentrism which conceived Christ's redemption exclusively under the aspect of expiation and satisfaction. The felicitous intuitions of Belluti in this connection mark an exception and are deserving of mention.

The unresolved tension we find in our authors is that between the *ordo amoris* and the *ordo justitiae*. According to Scotus' central perspective, the *ordo amoris* governs all divine actions *ad extra*. The theory of hamartiocentrism, on the contrary, is essentially grounded on the *ordo justitiae*. Our authors, as so many others, adopt the Scotistic perspective when they describe the mystery of the Incarnation, and so their thought is dominated by the *ordo amoris*. However, when they treat of the redemption, they follow the *ordo justitiae*. This explains why they are incapable of bringing together Incarnation and redemption in one single harmonious outlook. The famous theory of the two decrees is the inevitable—and untenable—result of all this.

The great need in this connection was an integration of the true elements in the *ordo justitiae* within the dominating and higher ambit of the *ordo amoris*. But this was very difficult at that time. To achieve that, our theologians needed a greater penetration of the sources of Revelation, a surmounting of the hamartiocentric mentality then prevalent, and an adequate understanding of the theory of satisfaction. Perhaps only an extraordinary theological genius could have accomplished this. Nevertheless, the very fact that they show us, to the point of evidence, that it was impossible to conciliate the two orders in one single design already contitutes a true progress. At least they indicate in what direction the solution can *not* be discovered, and so, by way of elimination, they stimulate us to search for it elsewhere.

7.

Concluding Observations

To a superficial observer, the foregoing discussion of Christ's universal primacy and its vicissitudes in the history of theology may appear to be a mere remembrance of a scholastic dispute over a marginal theological point. That is to say, it may appear interesting only as a historical curiosity. In effect, in our manuals of theology the problem is confined to the margin of Christology. It has an altogether secondary importance and has no bearing whatever on the development of Christological doctrine in general. In Christian anthropology, in the tracts on creation, on grace and ecclesiology there is not so much as an allusion to the primacy of Christ. In many theological treatises the matter is practically neglected even when the nexus between the Incarnation and soteriology is discussed.

It does not seem, however, that the question of Christ's primacy is only a medieval problem, or one representing a mere theological curiosity. It definitely is not a marginal doctrine. In our view, it constitutes the very heart and center of theology, the key to all the further elaborations and distinctions. After all, is it not *in* Christ Jesus that God has revealed Himself to us? And is it not *in* and *through* Christ Jesus that we are able to arrive at a coherent understanding of God, of man, of the universe? As a matter of fact, in recent times theological thought has given signs of becoming more and more aware of that truth, even though here and there we still notice an indecisive, tentative groping along these lines. To be sure, the medieval formulation of Christ's primacy must undergo a revision; especially the doctrine must be liberated from certain narrow horizons we have discussed above. It must be studied from a much broader perspective and in all its dimensions. But the doctrine in itself is anything but academic.

Taking into consideration the vast perspective proper to our doctrine, particularly in the context of recent theology, we would like to indicate briefly its reprecussions on the global overview of the theological discipline and on the principal facets thereof. We will limit ourselves to mere references, without any in-depth considerations which would lie beyond the scope of this essay.

1. The Theological Problem

There is no doubt that the influence of the Nominalists first, and of the Illuminists later, left a grave and lasting burden on the theological mentality and methodology of past centuries. Often this mentality still comes through especially in scholastic manuals. One of the most serious aspects of that influence is the pulverization of the contents of Revelation. We mean, specifically, that the great Christian mysteries of the Trinity, Incarnation, Redemption, Eschatology, Grace, etc. become ever more disjoined among themselves and are treated as isolated doctrines, as if they were loose and rambling blocks. They do not constitute a supernatural "order," an organism that is living and hence vitally connected, but rather a conglomerate of independent truths.

Already during the last century the "Tübingen School," with Prof. A. Möhler and especially the prominent Rhenish theologian Matthias J. Scheeben, had vigorously reacted against this tendency in the name of genuine Scholasticism, Sacred Scripture and the Fathers of the Church. Such protests have become even livelier and more widespread in more recent years. The search for the organicity and unitary vision of what Scheeben used to call the "supernatural Kosmos" is one of the essential tasks of Christian theology. After all, it is in the whole that the single parts unfold their due importance and are reciprocally illuminated. To achieve this was exactly the primary purpose of the "Sacra Doctrina" of the great Scholastics.

Now, the heart and foundation of Christian theology is, admittedly, Jesus Christ, the eternal Word made flesh. He is the Way, the Truth, and the Life for all generations. Absolutely no one comes to the Father except through Him. Jesus Christ is the light that illumines every man. Are these not the key assertions of St. John's Gospel?

All our theological knowledge is based on Christ, is dominated by Him, flows from His richness. Christology, then, is the clue to Christian theology, its starting point and its measure. It is the center from which all the lines proceed and on which they all converge. The "supernatural Kosmos" has its substance in Christ Jesus. As Pascal once wrote:

> Not only do we know God by Jesus Christ alone, but we know ourselves only by Jesus Christ. We know life and death only through Jesus Christ. Apart from Jesus Christ, we do not know what is our life, nor our

death, nor God, nor ourselves.[1]

And Prof. Karl Barth declares:

Tell me how it stands with your Christology, and I shall tell you who you are. This is the point at which ways diverge, and the point at which is fixed the relation between theology and philosophy, and the relation between knowledge of God and knowledge of men, the relation between revelation and reason, the relation between Gospel and law, the relation between God's truth and man's truth. . . . At this point everything becomes clear or unclear, bright or dark. For here we are standing at the center.[2]

St. Bonaventure had observed, many centuries earlier, that for the true Christian theologian always "incipiendum est a medio quod est Christus."[3] And the reason is that "Christus [est] unus omnium Magister."[4]

Now, the Incarnation is the essential, constitutive fact of the God-Man. But by being inserted in history, it assumes that which is proper to history, namely, that self-expansion toward the *eschaton*-fullness. That is why Christ's death, Resurrection and Ascension into Heaven cannot be considered as events disjoined from the Incarnation, as facts which exhaust in themselves their value and their significance. It is rather the Son of God made Man who, on His way to the *eschaton*, dies, comes back to life, returns to Heaven. The nexus, among the various mysteries of the life of Christ is, then, an ontological datum which finds its root and its explanation in the Incarnation. Hence, for the entire realm of Revelation, Christ represents the center, the keystone, the determining value. He alone imparts to it its plausible complexion. God, the world, man, grace and salvation must be seen and known *in* Christ, in the light of Christ, in a harmonious and illuminating unity. Thus the doctrine of His primacy and universal supremacy appear as the inspiration and the coagulating center of every sector of theology.

2. The Ecclesiological Problem

Ecclesiology is nothing but a projection of Christology. It stands to reason, then, that it should be elaborated and developed in light of Christ and of His primacy. Even a summary knowledge of history will reveal that every Christological error has profound repercussion on Ecclesiology. And the opposite is also true: every ecclesiological deviation presupposes a Christological error. After analyzing the Protestant Reformation with extraordinary insight, the eminent Prof. Möhler traced the entire process to this primordial deficiency: "Luther never understood the true value of these words: The Word became flesh, the Word became Man."[5] And yet, apparently, Luther never questioned the *fact* that God had become man. Karl Barth shares the same opinion. In his already-quoted words, "Tell me what your Christology is and I will tell you who you are," he is stressing the fact that every divergence among Christians is, basically, a Christological divergence. The "juridicist," fragmentary or extrinsicist concept of the Church which we can detect even in not a few Catholic theologians, especially during the post-Tridentine period, derives from a partial appreciation of Christology.

The well-balanced and complete elaboration of Ecclesiology must begin with an exact and complete Christology. The Second Vatican Council in its remarkable decrees on the Liturgy, the Church and Ecumenism teaches us a lesson in methodology which is of the highest importance along these lines.[6] Many decades ago, the Protestant theologian A. Deissman accurately foresaw that ours would be "the century of the Church." The great ecumenical endeavors which, under the influence of the Spirit, animate and stimulate all Christians constitute, above all else, a rediscovery of Christology as a discerning value. This has been frankly brought out by even many Orthodox and Protestant scholars in their ecumenical meetings.

In this field, too, which has incalculable consequences, the doctrine of Christ's primacy—the heart of Christology—has a significance and a bearing of vast proportions. It is indispensable in order to grasp adequately the teaching of Scripture concerning Christ. The great Epistles of St. Paul, particularly to the Ephesians and to the Colossians, have as their central theme precisely the doctrine of Christ's universal supremacy. This doctrine appears, therefore, as a premise of decisive moment even for an adequate elaboration of ecumenism. And ecumenism, in turn, will find in the common proclamation of Christ's primacy one of the indispensable openings to appreciate whatever elements of truth are ardently cherished by Orthodox and Protestants alike. It will find, in short, a common point of departure for an accurate understanding of the Church.

3. The Anthropological Problem

A field in which one feels the absolute urgency of a truly complete Christology—a Christology, that is, which is governed by the doctrine of Christ's primacy—is that of cosmology and anthropology. It is in this area that modern thought has impressed a decisive mark, managing to formulate a concept which seems impervious to Christianity.

Numerous scholars have emphasized how the profound scientific transformations and the concept itself of science have changed the mentality of contemporary man in a radical way, tearing him away from the centuries-old pattern of thinking. What we are dealing with is the relationship between God and the world, the doctrine of creation, and the sense of history, which is the consciousness of becoming, the consciousness of evolving.

It is a very grave situation, to be sure. And yet, man, though dominated by a technico-scientific civilization, is not irreligious and atheistic by nature; he is so because he does not know how to conciliate the scientific vision of the universe with a certain presentation of Christianity which is narrow and tied to a prop of human knowledge that has long been surpassed and transcended.

The well-known philosopher Gabriel Marcel once wrote:

> My most intimate and deeply-rooted conviction (and if it is heretical, too bad for orthodoxy) is that, regardless of all that may have been said by so many doctors and spiritual masters, God does not wish to be loved by us *against* creation, but that He wishes to be loved *through* creation, and using it as a point of departure. That is why I do not tolerate certain pious books. As far as I am concerned, a God who erects Himself against creation and is, as it were, jealous of His own works, is nothing but an idol.[7]

These rather harsh and excessive words express well the mentality of so many modern Christians who reject a spirituality that does not take earthly values into consideration.

Undoubtedly, serious theological deficiencies have contributed to this regrettable cleavage between Christianity and the modern world. In the first place, theological thought is still tied to a scientific vision of the world which is actually pre-Galilean. Now, it is a fact that no theology can prescind from a certain scientific vision of the world, at least as a terminus and point of insertion in history. And if it is true that it is physics that renders metaphysics obsolete, it is also undeniable that science can make our theology look antiquated. In effect, our theology must express itself in human categories, and thus it runs the risk of becoming totally incomprehensible if it is wrapped up in scientific (or pre-scientific) notions that have been surpassed for centuries. It cannot be denied that sometimes our theology is based on an infantile vision of the universe and wholly neglects the enormous changes that have occurred not only after Galileo, but even in recent decades.

An important feature of this change is the passage from a static to a dynamico-historical outlook. The effort to maintain a theology linked with a "Ptolomaic" scheme—whether we do it out of laziness, or traditionalism, or misguided loyalty—means simply to situate ourselves outside of history.

Theology must propose Christian truth, immutable in its essence, according to the mental categories and the world view of different historical epochs. In order to be fecund, theology must sink deep into the culture of the times.

It often happens that this static and archaic character of theology has brought about not only an impermeability between Christian truths and the modern world, but a real theological void in the culture of our times. As Cardinal Cushing, Archbishop of Boston, once said with characteristic bluntness:

> Theologians are playing with wind-mills; they have not sufficiently devoted themselves to the study of the difficult problems that separate science from faith. If science has sometimes minimized the importance of religion in the life of man, theology has too often ignored the achievements of science and has remained aloof from the risks of scientific research.[8]

Theology has not only not shown interest in the enormous efforts of science; it has often looked at them with detachment and even haughtiness, seeing in them something Promethean, a desecration of the world, almost feeling happy over the failures of scientific reserach, always ready to minimize its successes.

At the bottom of this attitude lies a woefully unsatisfactory notion of the relationship between creation and salvation, between Christ and the universe. More: the hamartiocentrism with which our theology (especially the spritual branch) is so often saturated, naturally tends to condemn the world as evil, thus setting the God-Redeemer against the God-Creator.

For this reason we affirm that the doctrine of Christ's primacy is indispensable for a correct evaluation of that relationship. In effect, for Christianity, God and the universe meet in Jesus Christ. The mystery of the divine will expressed in creation is revealed to us in Jesus Christ, center and terminus of every creature. Now, all our theology concerning man and the universe depends on the way we conceive the relationship between Christ and creation. If we think that the exclusive or primary purpose of Christ's existence was to repair an order which already existed without Him, that is, to heal the broken friendship between God and man, then of course we must separate creation from the Incarnation. In this fashion, we will have a creation whose original structure was "neutral," prescinding from Christ. Its relationship with Christ is established "later" and "ratione peccati." Obviously, this type of relationship is only extrinsic, juridico-moral. Consequently, creation does not enter, *per se,* the realm of salvation. In this kind of theology the universe will be seen merely as a premise of salvation; theology will be concerned with it only in order to verify, in light of Revelation, the purely rational knowledge man can have about it.

This is, regrettably, the usual treatment creation receives in our theology textbooks.[9] Within this framework it is impossible to outline a theology of creation without risking the danger of naturalism and seeing the world only as "the field of sin"—opposition to Christ. Only the universal primacy of Christ can overcome this deadly fracture and give us a true theology of "terrestrial reality" in conformity with the divine master-plan for salvation that can surmount the world "profanation" brought about by hamartiocentrism. The consequences of adopting this Christological point of departure are incalculable and have repercussions on the whole of theological anthropology. Finally, it will allow us to overcome that radical mentality which conceives of nature as opposed to grace. Sacred Scripture looks upon creation quite differently. Creation is not a neutral premise, but the first act of the "historia salutis" centered in Jesus Christ.

The thorough search along these lines conducted by recent exegesis has yielded very important and gratifying clarification.[10] It has brought to light the role that belongs to Christ in relation to creation according to Sacred Scripture. It has shown how creation is *within* the salvation design. And this perspective gives us the true criterion and the general principle for a theological anthropology and for a theology of terrestrial realities. Now, this supremely important general principle is precisely the biblical doctrine of Christ's absolute and universal primacy.

Unfortunately, our systematic theologians have not always taken into consideration the valuable contributions of our exegetes. The capital task of contemporary theology is precisely to describe the relationship between Christ "Alpha and Omega" and the universe, to illustrate the cosmic dimension of the Savior's role.

Another very serious problem clamoring for a satisfactory and adequate theological solution is that of the relationship between Christianity and non-Christian religions. In this field, too, which up to now has been treated in a superficial fashion, the doctrine of Christ's primacy is undoubtedly of decisive importance. It is the clue to an efficacious theological solution.

As can be seen, the entire realm of theology is profoundly conditioned by the doctrine of Christ's primacy. This problem is anything but the relic of a subtle and sterile controversy between two theological Schools. It constitutes a total option, a conception of Christianity, a focal point that irradiates literally everything.

If the theology of our times wishes to be faithful to its task and offer a satisfactory response to so many questions posed by the historical and

cultural situations of today's world, it must begin by coming face to face
with the key-problem of Jesus Christ's absolute and universal primacy:

"INCIPIENDUM EST A CHRISTO."

NOTES

¹ The literature on our subject is very vast. Here are some of the more important items: F. M. Risi, Ord. S.J. de Deo, *Sul motivo primario della Incarnazione del Verbo* . . . (Roma, 1897-1898) 4 vols.; Jean B. du Petit-Bornand, O.F.M.Cap., *Essai sur la primauté de Jésus-Christ et sur le motif de l'Incarnation* (Paris, 1900); Chrysostome Urrutibéhéty, O.F.M., *Le motif de l'Incarnation et les principaux thomistes contemporains* (Tours, 1921); J. F. Bonnefoy, O.F.M., *Il Primato di Cristo nella teologia contemporanea*, in *Problemi e Orientamenti di Teologia Dommatica* (Milano, 1957) II, 123-236; Id., *La Primauté du Christ selon l'Ecriture et la Tradition* (Rome, 1959), translated and abridged by M. D. Meilach, O.F.M.,and published under the title *Christ and the Cosmos* (Paterson, N.J., 1965); D. J. Unger, O.F.M.Cap., *Franciscan Christology. Absolute and Universal Primacy of Christ*, in *FS* 2 (1942) 428-448; Id., *Select Questions on the Final Cause of the Incarnation*, in *FEC* 38 (1957) 46-76; E. Rabbitte, O.F.M., *The Primacy of Christ. A Study in Speculative Theology*, in *IER* 70 (1948) 878-889; L. M. Bello, O.F.M., *De universali Christi primatu atque regalitate*, in *AOFM* 52 (1933) 293-311; J. B. Carol, O.F.M., *The Absolute Primacy and Predestination of Jesus and His Virgin Mother* (Chicago, Illinois, 1981).

² Cf. J. Gross, *La divinisation du chrétien d'après les Pères grecs* (Paris, 1938).

³ St. Maximus, *Ad Thalassium*, q. 60; PG 90, 620-621. Cf. D. J. Unger, *Christ Jesus, Center and Final Scope of all Creation, according to St. Maximus Confessor*, in *FS* 9 (1949) 50-62.

⁴ On St. Anselm, cf. J. Rivière, *Le Dogme de la Rédemption. Essai d'étude historique* (Paris, 1905) 104-105; Id., *Le Dogme de la Rédemption au début du Moyen-Age* (Paris, 1934) 292-403; J. McIntyre, *St. Anselm and His Critics, A Re-interpretation of the "Cur Deus Homo"* (Edimburg, 1954); M. Richard, *Le mystère de la Rédemption* (Tournai, 1959) 131ff.

⁵ To evaluate exactly St. Anselm's "rationes necessariae" we should bear in mind that he does not consider the matter from the viewpoint of pure reason; he starts out from faith so as to be able to capture in it the nexus which binds the various revealed truths.

[6] St. Anselm, *Cur Deus Homo*, I, cc. 14-15.

[7] Op. cit., I, cc. 11-19.

[8] Op. cit., I, c. 23.

[9] Ibid.

[10] Op. cit., II, cc. 4-9.

[11] Op. cit., II, cc. 10-19.

[12] Cf. Rivière, *Le Dogme de la Rédemption au début du Moyen-Age*, 291.

[13] Thus M. Richard, op. cit., 136.

[14] G. Oggioni, *Il mistero della redenzione*, in *Problemi e Orientamenti di Teologia Dommatica* (Milano, 1957) II, 277.

[15] St. Cyril of Alexandria, *Thesaurus*, assert. 15; *PG* 75, 288. Cf. Unger, *Christ Jesus, the Secure Foundation, according to St. Cyril of Alexandria*, in *FS* 7 (1947) 1-25; 324-343; 399-414; G. Basetti-Sani, O.F.M., *Il Primato di Cristo in San Cirillo*, in *Kyrilliana, Spicilegia edita S. Cyrilli Alexandrini XV recurrente saeculo* [444-1944] (Le Caire, 1947) 139-196.

[16] Rupert of Deutz, *De gloria et honore filii hominis*, lib. 3; *PL* 168, 1628-1629.

[17] Cf. Carol, op. cit., 19-20.

[18] The *Summa Theologica fratris Alexandri*, attributed during so many centuries to Alexander of Hales, seems to have been written, according to recent scholars, by John de la Rochelle (books I and III), William of Melitona (book IV) and a third author (book II perhaps by Eudes Rigaud). These authors drew their material from the works of Alexander of Hales and also from their own writings. Probably Alexander inspired the plan of the work. The *Summa Fratris Alexandri* has been critically edited and published at Quaracchi, 1924ff. Cf. E. Gössmann, *Metaphysik und Heilsgeschichte. Eine theologische Untersuchung der Summa Halensis* (München, 1964).

[19] "If therefore the highest diffusion ought to belong to Him, since He is the Highest Good, it is more appropriate that He should diffuse Himself into creatures. But this diffusion cannot be understood to be the highest unless He Himself be united to the creature. Therefore, it is fitting that God should be united to a creature, and especially to man, as has been shown. Therefore, supposing that man were not fallen, the highest Good would still be united to him." Alexander of Hales, *Summa Theologica*, lib. III, tr. I, q. 2, tit. 2; *Op. omn.* (Ad Claras Aquas, 1948) IV, 4.

[20] Loc. cit.; IV, 41-42.

[21] Loc, cit.; IV, 42. The author is here commenting on a text of St. Bernard on the words "Propter me orta est tempestas" (Jonas 1:12); cf. *PL* 183, 37.

[22] "It is to be conceded that even if human nature were not fallen, still the Incarnation would be fitting." Loc. cit.; IV, 42: *Respondeo*.

[23] Alexander, op. cit., lib. III, tr. I, q. 3, c. 5: *Op. omn.* IV, 46-47.

[24] St. Bonaventure, In III Sent, d. 1, a. 2, q. 1; *Op. omn.* (Ad Claras Aquas, 1887) III, 19-21.

[25] "It appears that the work of Incarnation was most fitting to divine piety." Ibid.

²⁶ In II Sent., d. 1, p. II, a. 2, q. 1.

²⁷ " . . . is the multiple perfection arising from the dignity of that work. For the Incarnation works toward the perfection of man and consequently, toward the perfection of the whole universe, in that it completes and gives completion to mankind, according to what regards nature, to what regards grace, and to that which regards glory." In III Sent., d. 1, a. 2, q. 2: *Conclusio; Op. Omn.* III, 23.

²⁸ Loc. cit.

²⁹ "Which of these two opinions is more true is known to Him Who deigned to become Incarnate for us. But it is difficult to see which of these should be preferred, since both are in accordance with Catholic belief, and both are held by Catholics. Both opinions also, according to difference considerations, are conducive to devotion." Loc. cit.; III, 24.

³⁰ From Sacred Scripture, St. Bonaventure cites Matth. 18; Gal. 4:45. From the Fathers, he refers to St. Augustine and St. Bernard.

³¹ " . . . it is more consonant with the piety of faith, it honors God more, it more acclaims the mystery of the Incarnation; and it more ardently influences our affection." Loc. cit.; III, 25.

³² ". . . signifies the uniting of Christ with the Church." Loc. cit.; III, 22-23.

³³ "He made man for this reason, because he foresaw that he would be in need of redemption; and therefore the more principal intention was the reparation of fallen man, rather than his condition of a possible fall." For a detailed examination of the solutions given by St. Bonaventure to these arguments, cf. Risi, op. cit., I, 21ff.

³⁴ Cf. In III Sent., d. 13, a. 2, q. 3.

³⁵ " . . . for it signifies the conjunction of God with the Church according to love, and it signifies also a conjunction according to union in the unity of the person." These tracts are published in vol. V of the *Opera omnia.*

³⁶ Thus J. G. Bourgerol, O.F.M., *Introduction à l'étude de St. Bonaventure* (Paris, 1961) 126.

³⁷ Cf. Bourgerol, ibid. Concerning St. Bonaventure's viewpoint on our question, see Z. Hayes, O.F.M., *The Life and Christological Thought of St. Bonaventure,* in *Franciscan Christology,* ed. D. McElrath (Fanciscan Institute, St. Bonaventure University, 1980) 67, note 16; Id., *Incarnation and Creation in the Theology of St. Bonaventure,* in *Studies Honoring Ignatius Charles Brady, Friar Minor,* ed. Almagno-Harkins (Franciscan Institute, St. Bonaventure, N.Y., 1976) esp. 328, where the author writes that the opinion of the Seraphic Doctor on the reason for the Incarnation is frequently misread.

³⁸ St. Thomas, In III Sent., d. 1., q. 1. aa. 3-4; d. 43, a. 2; *De Veritate,* q. 29, a. 4; *Comment, in 1 Tim.,* 1; *Summa Theologica* III, q. 1, a. 3.

³⁹ Thus H. M. Féret, O.P., *A propos de la primauté du Christ,* in *RSPT* 27 (1938) 69-70; 112.

⁴⁰ We say "some" patristic texts because this is not the most frequent manner of expression in the Fathers when they touch on this question, not even in those who, like St. Augustine, use it explicitly. Cf. A. Spindeler, *Cur Verbum*

caro factum? *Das Motiv der Menschwerdung und das Verhältnis der Erlösung zur Menschwerdung Gottes in den christologischen Glaubenskämpfen des vierten und fünften christlichen Jahrhunderts* (München, 1936).

[41] St. Augustine; *PL* 38, 940.

[42] "I answer that in this question the truth can only be known by Him who, because He Himself willed it, was born and offered in sacrifice." St. Thomas, In III Sent., d. 1, q. 1, a. 3.

[43] St. Thomas, *Summa Theologica*, III, q. 1, a. 3.

[44] "Since in Holy Scripture the explanation of the Incarnation is always given from man's original sin, it is more fittingly said that God ordained the Incarnation as a rememdy for sin, so that if sin had not existed, the Incarnation would not have come about. Ibid.

[45] Loc. cit., ad 3m, 4m et 5m.

[46] "Others indeed say that since through the Incarnation of the Son of God is accomplished not only the liberation from sin, but also the exaltation of human nature and perfection of the whole universe, the Incarnation would have come about because of these reasons even if there were no sin; and this can be sustained as probable." In III Sent., d. 1, a. 3. *Respondeo dicendum.*

[47] Risi, op. cit., I, 35.

[48] St. Thomas himself tells us the weight to be given to dubious, probable, and certain propositions. Cf. *Summa*, II-II, q. 2, a. 9.

[49] St. Thomas, *Summa Theol.*, III, q. 8, aa. 3-4.

[50] Cf. *De Veritate*, q. 22, a. 8; *Contra Gent.*, III, 88; *Summa Theol.*, I-II, q. 9, a. 6. For a good explanation of the views held by St. Thomas on the "motive" of the Incarnation, cf. M.D. Meilach, O.F.M., *St. Thomas Aquinas and the Primacy of Christ*, in *Int* 1 (N. 1, 1960) 22-27; also Chrysostome [Urrutibéhéty], op. cit., 417-443.

[51] Cf. Risi, op. cit., I, 35.

[52] For a critico-theological evaluation of the pertinent matter, cf. I. Biffi, *Un bilancio delle recenti discussioni sul piano della Summa Theologiae*, in *ScCatt*, Suppl. 2 (1963) 147-176, and Suppl. 3 (1963) 295-326.

[53] M. D. Chenu, O.P., *St. Thomas d'Aquin et la théologie* (Paris, 1959).

[54] A. Hayen, O.P., *St. Thomas d'Aquin et la vie de L'Eglise* (Louvain, 1952).

[55] E. Pérsson, *Le plan de la Somme Théologique et le rapport "Ratio-Revelatio*," in *RPL* 56 (1958) 545-572.

[56] Cf. Persson, art. cit., 563.

[57] Persson, art. cit., 553.

[58] E. Gilson, in *BT* 8 (1953) 10.

[59] Y. Congar, O.P., *La foi et la théologie* (Tournay, 1962) 203-205.

[60] L. Ciappi, O.P., *Il motivo dell'Incarnzione e "Les deux Adam" di P. Galtier*, in *Spz* 3 (1950) 103-104.

CHAPTER II

[1] Besides the works mentioned at the beginning of Chapter I, cf. O. Schäfer,

Bibliographia de vita, operibus et doctrina Joannis Duns Scoti, Doctoris Subtilis et Mariani, saec, XIX-XX (Romae, 1954); Id., *Conspectus brevis bibliographiae scotisticae recentioris,* in *AOFM,* 85 (1966) 531-550; W. Hoeres, *Der Wille als reine Vollkommenheit nach Duns Scotus* (München, 1962), an indispensable work to understand our subject properly; J. Klein, *Die Charitaslehre des Johannes Duns Skotus* (München, 1936); P. Hercedez, *La place du Christ dans le plan de la création selon le B. Jean Duns Scot,* in *FF* 19 (1936) 30-52; C. Balić, *Duns Skotus Lehre über Christi Prädestination im Lichte der neuersten Forschungen,* in *WuW* 3 (1936) 19-35; Id., *La prédestination de la Très-Sainte Vierge dans la doctrine de Jean Duns Scot,* in *FF* 19 (1936) 114-158; Raymond de Courcerault, O.F.M. Cap., *Le motif de l'Incarnation: Duns Scot et l'Ecole scotiste,* in *FF* 28 (1912) 186-201; 313-331; A. Martini, O.F.M., *Sul motivo primario dell'Incarnazione* in *SF* 6 (1934) 3-33; 288-318; A. B. Wolter, O.F.M., *John Duns Scotus on the Primacy and Personality of Christ,* in *Franciscan Christology* (St. Bonaventure, N.Y., 1980) 139-182, esp. 140-142; Id., *Duns Scotus on the Predestination of Christ,* in *Crd* 5 (Dec., 1955) 366-371; L. Veuthey. O.F.M. Conv., *De ratione Incarnationis,* in *MF* 41 (1941) 97-102; A. Sanna, O.F.M.Conv., *Le regalità di Cristo secondo la Scuola francescana* (Oristano, 1951); J. Bissen, O.F.M., *De praedestinatione absoluta Christi secundum Duns Scotum expositio doctrinalis,* in *Ant* 12 (1937) 3-36. For further literature, see J. B. Carol, O.F.M., *The Absolute Primacy and Predestination of Jesus and His Virgin Mother* (Chicago, 1981) 96-144.

[2] On Scotus' idea of will and freedom, which a hostile tradition always tries to present as being a blind voluntarism, see the exhaustive and admirable work by W. Hoeres, cited in the previous footnote. Also B. M. Bonansea, O.F.M., *Duns Scotus' Voluntarism,* in *John Duns Scotus,* 1265-1965, ed. Ryan-Bonansea (The Catholic University of America Press, Washington, D.C., 1965) 83-121. On the problem of contingency, see P. Scapin, O.F.M. Conv., *Contingenza e libertà in Giovanni Duns Scoto* (Roma, 1964).

[3] It seems incredible that a scholar like Th.-A. Audet, O.P., in his article *Approches historiques de la Summa Theologiae,* in *EHLD* (Montréal-Paris, 1962) 7-29, sees in Scotus' solution to the problem of Christ's primacy an application of the naturalistic, Neoplatonic axiom, *Bonum diffusivum sui,* in the sense of a necessary communication on the part of God. It so happens that Scotus, more radically than any other theologian, refuted the Greco-Aristotelian necessitarism and stressed the notion of divine freedom. The will, whether human or divine, is always and essentially free. Another remarkable statement by the same author is to the effect that Franciscan theology is "une liquidation implicite de toute l'histoire sainte de la Bible" (p. 28).

[4] "But here there are two doubts. First whether this predestination (i.e., of Christ) necessarily presupposes the fall of human nature; many authorities appear to say this." John Duns Scotus, *Ordinatio,* III, d. 3, q. 3; critical ed. by C. Balić, O.F.M., *Joannis Duns Scoti, Doctoris Mariani, Theologiae Marianae elementa* (Sibenici, 1933) 4.

[5] "Predestination is the foreordaining of some being principally to glory, and to other things insofar as they are ordered to glory." Scotus, loc. cit.; ed. Balić, 2.

[6] St. Thomas, *Summa Theol.*, I, q. 23, a. 1.

[7] "Much more is this true of the predestination of that soul which was predestined to the highest glory." Scotus, loc. cit.; ed. Balić 5.

[8] "For, universally, he who wills in an orderly manner seems to will first that which is more proximate to the end. Thus, just as [God] first wills that someone should receive glory before [He wills that he should receive] grace, so also among the predestined, to whom He wills glory, He seems ordinately to will first the glory of him whom He wills to be proximate to the end, and thus He wills the glory of this soul [of Christ] before that of some other soul, and He wills the glory and grace of anyone before He foresees the things that are opposed to these habits." Scotus, ibid.

[9] Freedom, which is inseparable from every act of the will, is not, for Scotus, as it is for St. Thomas, a capacity to choose, a pure indifference toward various alternatives, which follows the last judgment of reason. According to this idea, the clearer our understanding, the evidence, the more does freedom diminish. Faith is free because it is "obscure"; in Heaven the beatific act of the will will no longer be free because of the beatific vision, etc. For Scotus, on the contrary, the clearer our understanding, the freer the act of the will. That is why our freedom will reach its perfection only in Heaven. Freedom, in its absolute value, exists in the infinite act by which God wills and loves Himself. Obviously, the two concepts are profoundly different. Cf. W. Hoeres, op. cit., 86ff.; 297ff.

[10] "As universally freedom is compatible with foreknowledge, so perfect freedom is compatible with the most perfect foreknoweldge." Scotus, In I Sent., Prol. q. 4. n. 34.

[11] W. Hoeres, op. cit., 91.

[12] Scotus, *Opus Par.* III, d. 7, q. 4; ed. Balić, 14-15. Cf. also *Ordinatio*, III, d. 19, q. un. On the authenticity of this last *quaestio*, cf. Balić, art. cit., in *WuW* 3 (1936) 20.

[13] Cf. Scapin, op. cit., 16ff. Scotus never ceases repeating that "voluntas est potentia libera per essentiam," as opposed to all other forms of causality. *In Metaphys.* IX, c. 15, n. 4; *Collat.* 16, n. 8.

[14] Those who are utterly ignorant of Scotus' teaching very often portray him as a proponent of blind voluntarism; but when it suits his critics, the Subtle Doctor is portrayed as a proponent of the Greek necessitarism. Thus, to limit ourselves to the question of Christ's primacy, G. Martelet, in his article *Sur le motif de l'Incarnation*, in *Problèmes actuels de Christologie*, ed. Bouëssé-Latour (Desclée de Brouwer, 1961) 42, writes: "Postulée comme le premier contenu des décrets divins, en fonction des exigences de diffusion du Bien suprème, l'Incarnation peut apparaître dans le scotisme comme une sorte de réalité métaphysique, metahistorique, intemporelle de droit, premier intelligible à interpreter dans une

logique absolue de las diffusion du bien.'' The author praises Th.-A. Audet (ref. above, note 3) for having profoundly understood "la logique de la position de Scot à partir du principe neo-platonicien du *Bonum diffusivum sui*" (p. 41, note). It is difficult to understand how so many false ideas can be attributed to Scotus in such a short sentence. The least that we can expect of Scotus' critics is that they give us an objective presentation of his thought, and not a convenient caricature thereof.

¹⁵ Father George [Payne], O.F.M., *Incarnation is Complement of Creation: the Duns Scotus View*, in *ER* 88 (May, 1933) 522-526.

¹⁶ Hence, Prof. B. Bartmann is absolutely wrong when he accuses Scotus of teaching the abstract *necessity* of the Incarnation (even *Adamo non peccante*) for the perfection of the universe. Cf.his *Lehrbuch der Dogmatik*, 7th ed. (Freiburg im Breisgau, 1928) I, 313. The accusation is repeated in his *Manuale di Teologia Dogmatica*, tr. from the 8th German edition (Alba, 1949) II, 15. Bartmann is wrong on three counts: *first*, because Scotus has, more than anybody else, stressed God's absolute freedom in His works *ad extra*; *secondly*, because Scotus has *never* written a word about the Incarnation being the perfection of the universe, but says the very opposite; and *thirdly*, because Scotus *never* treats our question in the abstract, but always in the present, concrete order.

¹⁷ Scotus, *Ordinatio*, III, d. 7, q. 3; ed. Balić, 7.

¹⁸ "It seems that the 'instants [of reason]' of Scotus should be banished." L. Molina, S.J., *Commentaria in Primam Divi Thomae Partem* . . . , q. XXIII, aa. IV-V, disp. I, memb. 7 (ed. Venetiis, 1594) I, 334.

¹⁹ L. Ciappi, O.P., *Il motivo dell'Incarnazione e "Les deux Adam" di P. Galtier*, in *Spz* 3 (1950) 104.

²⁰ St. Thomas, *Summa Theol.*, I, q. 20, a. 1.

²¹ St. Francis de Sales, *Treatise on the Love of God*, II, 5; tr. H. B. Mackey (Westminster, Md., 1942) 76.

²² "First we must see that according to Anselm, it was necessary for man to be redeemed. Second, that he could not be redeemed without satisfaction. Third that the satisfaction was to be accomplished by the God-man. Fourth, that the more fitting mode was this, namely through Christ's passion." Scotus, In III Sent., d. 20, q. un.; ed. Vivès (Parisiis, 1894) XIV, 737.

²³ "All these things which were accomplished by Christ concerning our redemption were not necessary except on the presupposition that the divine or-dination ordained that it should come about in this way, and then it was only necessary by consequent necessity that Christ should suffer; but nevertheless the whole was simply speaking contingent, both the antecedent and the conse-quent." Scotus, loc. cit.

²⁴ "Given that man might have been redeemed in another way, while yet God by His free will redeemed him thus, we are bound to Him much more than if there had been no other way in which we might have been redeemed." Scotus, loc. cit.; XIV, 738.

²⁵ "If we wish to salvage the position of Anselm, we may say that his

arguments proceed upon the presupposition of divine ordination which has ordained that man should be redeemed in this way; . . . nevertheless there was no necessity." Scotus, ibid.

[26] "All of the authorities can be explained as meaning that Christ would not have come as redeemer unless man had fallen, nor perhaps as passible." Scotus, *Ordinatio*, III, d. 7, q. 3; ed. Balić, 5-6.

[27] "It was principally in order to attract us to His Love, as I believe, that this came about, and because God willed that men should be more fully drawn to Him." Scotus, In III Sent., d. 20, q. un.; ed. Vivès, XIV, 738. The strength of Scotus demonstration is based on his idea of contigency. Wherever there is contingency (i.e., in any and everything which is not God), we must put divine freedom as the cause and the "ultimum principium resolutivum," but never necessity, because "nulla causatio alicujus causae potest salvare contingentiam, nisi Causa prima ponatur immediate contingenter causare" (In I Sent., d. 39, q. un., a. 2, n. 12). On this point, which separates Scotus considerably from St.Thomas, see Scapin, op. cit., 24ff.

[28] It is opportune to recall here Scotus' clarifying teaching on the relationship between sin and redemption. The Anselmian tradition, which St. Thomas made his own, affirms that the Incarnation was necessary in the hypothesis that God demanded a condign reparation for sin. The reason for this is that sin, as St. Thomas writes, possesses a certain infinite malice inasmuch as it is an offense against the infinite Person of God (*Summa Theol.*, III, q. 1, a. 2, ad 2m). For this reason no mere creature is capable of offering to God a condign satisfaction for sin. But Scotus questions this thesis, for more reasons than one. According to him, sin does not possess an infinite gravity. A mere creature, endowed by God with "summa gratia," could have satisfied *de condigno* for sin, if God had so desired. The connection, therefore, between sin and the redemption performed by Christ is extrinsic; it depends on God's will; it is not demanded by any intrinsic exigency, not even for a condign satisfaction. Like the Incarnation, the Redemption is the sheer manifestation of God's love. Cf. Scotus, *Ord.*, III, q. 20, n. 20. In Scotus' mind, the *ordo amoris* is truly dominating in every moment of Christ's life; everything is the expression of the free and gratuitous love of God and of the love of Christ.

[29] In this connection, J. Bissen observes quite correctly: "Haec quaestio [Christi praedestinationis] potest considerari vel seorsim et in se vel in conjunctione cum alia de motivo Incarnationis. Primo modo invenitur tractata apud A. Halensem . . . , St. Bonaventuram . . . , et S. Thomam . . . , nec ulla videtur apud illos Auctores specialis poni relatio unius quaestionis ad aliam. Secundo modo habetur apud Pecham, praesertim vero apud Scotum qui quaestionem de motivo Incarnationis modo patenti ut quaestionem secundariam ad aliam principalem de praedestinatione Christi introducit." Bissen, art. cit., in *Ant* 12 (1937) 4.

[30] In order to understand the nature of the love of God, St. Thomas makes this important observation: "Voluntas nostra non est causa bonitatis rerum, sed

ab ea movetur sicut ab objecto; amor noster, quo bonum alicui volumus, non est causa bonitatis ipsius, sed e converso bonitas ejus vel vera vel aestimata provocat amorem quo ei volumus et bonum conservare, quod habet et addi quod non habet; et ad hoc operamur. Sed amor Dei est infundens et creans bonitatem in rebus." Cf. *Summa Theol.*, I, q. 20, a. 2.

[31] Cf. M. Schulzetenberg, *The Teaching of Duns Scotus on the Incarnation*, in *HPR* (Feb., 1983) 6-7. He was answered by J. B. Carol, O.F.M., *Duns Scotus on the Incarnation*, in *HPR* (June, 1983) 4.

[32] See, for example, J. Rivière, *Le Dogme de la Rédemption au début du Moyen-Age* (Paris, 1934) *conclusion*.

[33] Cf. M. Miguens, O.F.M., *Base escriturística de la doctrina de Escoto sobre el primado de Cristo*, in *ASCSI* III (Romae, 1968) 105-167.

CHAPTER III

[1] Cajetan explains his views in his *Commentarium in III Partem Summae Theologiae*, q. 1, a. 3; published in *Sancti Thomae Aquinatis opera omnia* (ed. Leonina, Romae, 1803) XI, 15-16.

[2] Cajetan, loc. cit., p. 16, n. VI.

[3] Cajetan, loc. cit., p. 15, n. VI.

[4] "Since sins pertain partly to the order of nature and partly to the order of grace as opposed thereto, it results that the predestination of Christ to be the Son of God presupposes the prevision of future sins inasmuch as they refer to the presupposed orders in the genus of material cause." Cajetan, loc. cit., p. 16, n. VI.

[5] "Since the Incarnation we find in Scripture is only a redemptive one, we say that although God could have willed a future Incarnation even without Redemption, nonetheless he did not in fact will it except thus; since He Himself has not otherwise revealed His will, which can be known only from His own Revelation." Cajetan, loc. cit., p. 16, n. IX.

[6] "I believe that this commentary of Cajetan is so false that—not to jeopardize the honor which is owed to him—I do not judge his opinion to merit discussion. . . . In fact I am reluctantly drawn to consider such opinions, but the effort must be undertaken for the sake of those who judge him to be an oracle." A. Catarino, O.P., *Pro eximia praedestinatione Christi annotatio specialis in Commentaria Domini Cajetani* (Romae, 1551); reproduced by Risi, op. cit., I, 124-128.

[7] F. Suárez, S.J., *De Incarnatione*, disp. V, sectio 1, n. 3; *Op. omnia* (Parisiis, 1860) XVI, 198.

[8] Risi, op. cit., I, 116.

[9] In this connection, one must ask: To which stage—nature, grace, hypostatic order—does the *humanity* of Christ belong, according to Cajetan? Christ's is a true and perfect humanity like ours. Hence, God must have willed it in the order of nature, that is to say, before grace and the hypostatic union. He could

not have foreseen it and willed it as subsistent, as a finite person, for in that case it could not be subsequently assumed by the Word. It follows that God foresaw and willed Christ's humanity as united to the Word from the very beginning. "Therefore," Father Risi observes correctly, "Cajetan's fictitious world goes up in smoke, because either it does not contain all the natural elements, which is against (Cajetan's) hypothesis, or it includes the natural united (to the Word), which is against the purpose for which it was made." Op. cit., I, 117.

10 "Nor is it absurd that God should have foreseen the fall of Adam before He predestined Christ: just as it is not absurd that God should have foreseen a running hare and future monsters and other such things belonging to the order of nature before He predestined Christ." Cajetan, loc. cit., p. 16, n. X, *ad sextum*.

11 "The end obtains primacy among the other causes, and it is from the end that all the other causes become causes in act; for the agent does not act except for the sake of an end." St. Thomas, *Contra Gent.*, III, 17.

12 R. Garrigou-Lagrange is clear on this point: "Haec distinctio [the three orders of Cajetan] data est a Cajetano hic, et quamvis non omnia ab eo ibidem dicta (de ordinatione decretorum divinorum circa tres ordines naturae, gratiae et unionis hypostaticae) forte sint vera, attamen haec distinctio servanda est et servata est a sequentibus thomistis." Cf. *De Christo Salvatore* (Torino, 1945) 61.

13 Cajetan remains strictly within St. Thomas' principles. The current discussions concerning the plan of the *Summa* and the grave problems posed by it represent the same positions and difficulties which we have found in Cajetan, namely: a theology of the world and of grace without Christ; the role of Christ reduced to that of a means to bring about our "reditus in Deum"; the succession of orders and finalities; and the consequent extrinsic character of the supernatural's relation to the natural. Prof. E. Gilson, who is unquestionably a competent exponent of Thomistic thought, has observed in this connection: "Qui rougit d'aller jusque-là, manque l'essentiel de la théologie thomiste, rougit de saint Thomas d'Aquin." Cf. *BT* 8 (1947-1953) 9-10. For a good discussion of the weaknesses of Cajetan's theory, cf. Chrysostome [Urrutibéhéty], *Le motif de l'Incarnation et les principaux thomistes contemporains* (Tours, 1921) 102-114 and 165.

14 The Salmanticenses labored for over fifty years to prepare their famous *Cursus Theologicus*; it is rightly considered the most exhaustive and important production of the Thomistic School in the seventeenth century. On the history of this work, its various authors, its several editions, etc., see the definitive brochure of Enrique del Sagrado Corazón [Llamas], O.C.D., *Los Salmanticenses: Su vida y su obra* (Madrid, 1955). The tract on the Incarnation was written by Father John of the Annunciation, O.C.D. (d. 1701) and was first published in Lyons, 1687. In the better-known Palmé edition (Paris, 1879) the tract on the Incarnation is found in volume XIII. The Scotistic thesis to the effect that Christ is the *primum volitum* is endorsed on pp. 266-267; the Thomistic view is defended on pp. 269ff.

15 Salmanticenses, *Cursus Theologicus*, tomus IX, tractatus XXI: *De Incarnatione*, disp. II, dub. I, n. 8; ed. cit., XIII, 270. For further details see the

informative and thoughtful disquisition by Enrique del Sagrado Corazón, O.C.D., *Juan Duns Escoto en la doctrina de los Salmanticenses sobre el motivo de la Encarnación*, in *ASCSI* IV (Romae, 1968) 461-515.

[16] "The Incarnation would be prior to our salvation as a *finis cuius gratia*; but our salvation is prior as a *finis cui* and according to the notion of material cause." Salmanticenses, op. cit., disp. II, dub. I, n. 5; XIII, 268. Cf. Garrigou-Lagrange, O.P., *Le principe de finalité*, in *RTh* 4 (1921) 419ff. In several of his works the author defends the solution given by the Salmanticenses as the most complete and well-balanced presentation of the Thomistic thought on the subject.

[17] P. Galtier, S.J., *Les deux Adam* (Paris, 1947) 102, note.

[18] Risi, op. cit., I, 317. For a good refutation of the theory of the Salmanticenses, see Chrysostome [Urrutibéhéty], op. cit., 124-149; also Jean-Baptiste du Petit-Bornand, O.F.M.Cap., *Essai sur la primauté de Jésus-Christ et sur le motif de l'Incarnation* (Paris, 1900) 317-320.

[19] L. Thomassin, *Dogmata Theologica*, III: *De Incarnatione*, lib. 2, cc. 4-11 (ed. Parisiis, 1866) 189-249.

[20] "Primarily and of itself, the Incarnation of the Word and the predestination of the Word to become incarnate bespeak nothing other than an emptying of Himself and a stooping from divine loftiness to the lowest state."Thomassin, loc. cit., c. 6, n. VIII; ed. cit., III, 200.

[21] "It is most unusual for love to dare such a thing, unless it be in order to assist the fallen, to aid a friend in dire need." Thomassin, loc. cit., c. 7, n. XIV; ed. cit., III, 210. For St. Thomas' definition of mercy, cf. *Summa Theol.*, I, q. 21, a. 3.

[22] Garrigou-Lagrange, *De Christo Salvatore* (Torino, 1945) 69. For a fairly recent exposition of Thomistic thought, cf. A. Michel, art. *Incarnation* in *DTC* 7 (1921) 1445-1539, esp. 1501- 1505; M. Corvez, O.P., *Le motif de l'Incarnation*, in *RTh* 49 (1949) 103-121; H.M. Féret, O.P., *Creati in Christo Jesu*, in *SPT* 1 (1941-1942) 96-132; H. Bouëssé, O.P., *Le Sauveur du monde* (Chambery, 1951); Th.-A. Audet, O.P., *Approches historiques de la Summa Theolgiae*, in *EHLD* (Montréal-Paris, 1962) 7-29.

[23] In *Ang* 7 (1930) 289-302. This was answered by Fr. Chrysostome in *FF* 14 (1931) 113-168, esp. 159-165.

[24] Romae, 1930.

[25] St. Thomas, *Summa Theol.*, I, q. 19, a. 1, ad 3m; q. 20, a. 2.

[26] St. Thomas, *Summa Theol.*, I, q. 19, a. 2, ad 2m.

[27] St. Thomas, *Summa Theol.*, I, q. 20, a. 3.

[28] St. Augustine, *Tract. in Joannem*, CX.

[29] St. Thomas, *Summa Theol.* II--II, q. 30, a. 1.

[30] St. Thomas, *Summa Theol.*, I, q. 21, a. 3.

[31] A. Salmerón, S.J. (d. 1595), suggests that mercy need not presuppose a present misery; it may be applied to prevent a possible misery. Mercy, then, is not only "post peccatum, sed etiam ante; miseratio enim non solum est de

malo quod est, sed etiam de eo quod potest esse." Cf. his *Disputationes in Epistolas D. Pauli*; in 1 Tim., cap. 1, disp. 3; *Opera omnia* (Coloniae Agrippinae, 1615) XV, 434.

[32] "Of sin, considered as sin, Thomists say that it was the *occasion* of the Incarnation; and of sin, considered as being in need of remedy, they say that it was the cause or motive, or the reason and condition *sine qua non* of the Incarnation." Garrigou-Lagrange, *De motivo Incarnationis*, in *APAR* 10 (Romae, 1945) 34.

[33] C. V. Héris, O.P., *Il mistero di Cristo*, tr. from the 2nd French edition (Brescia, 1945) 32.

[34] Héris, op. cit., 31-32.

[35] Héris, op. cit., 33. In his *Le motif de l'Incarnation*, in *BSFEM* 4 (1938) 34, the author writes: "Le Christ est la fin de l'intention divine conditionnée *dans sa réalisation effective* par la rédemption des hommes."

[36] Cardinal Eugenio Pacelli, Sermon on the occasion of the 70th anniversary of the Association of Our Lady of a Happy Death on Nov. 28, 1937; cf. *Discorsi e Panegirici*, ed. 2 (Milano, 1939) 633.

[37] "The imperfect is always for the sake of the more perfect, and the more ignoble part for the sake of the more noble." St. Thomas, *Summa Theol.*, I, q. 105, a. 5.

[38] St. Cyril of Alexandria, *Thesaurus*, XV; *PG* 75, 258. Cf. D. J. Unger, O.F.M. Cap., *Christ Jesus, The Secure Foundation, according to St. Cyril of Alexandria* in *FS* 7 (1947) 1-25; 324-343; 399-414.

[39] Cf. Bonnefoy, *Il Primato* . . . , 189-206.

[40] Scotus, *Opus Par.*, III, d. 7, q. 4; ed. Balić, 14-15.

[41] On this cf. Bonnefoy, op. cit., 213ff.

[42] Cf. Th. Déman, O.P., art. *Salamanque* (Théologiens de), in *DTC* 14 (Paris, 1939) 1030.

[43] Féret, art. cit., in *SPT* 1 (1941-1942) 99.

[44] Garrigou-Lagrange, art. cit., in *APAR* 10 (1945) 17.

[45] Bouëssé, op. cit., 130. On this author, see the very important article by Bonnefoy, *Un essai recent sur le plan divin de la création*, in *MF* 52 (1952) 425-460; published also separately (Paris, 1953).

[46] M. Corvez, O.P. is an exception. He absolutely denies that Christ has a primacy of finality. Cf. his already mentioned article in *RTh* 49 (1949) 103-121.

[47] Bonnefoy, *Il Primato* . . . , 215.

[48] E. Hugon, O.P., *Le motif de l'Incarnation*, in *RTh* 21 (1913) 281.

[49] Bonnefoy, *Il Primato* . . . , 217.

[50] "Christ as man was not Head of our first innocent parents according to essential grace." Garrigou-Lagrange, *De Christo Salvatore* (Taurini, 1945) 233.

[51] "Christ as man did not communicate essential grace and glory to the angels." Garrigou-Lagrange, op. cit., 241.

[52] "Nor is it necessary that the moral head of the angels communicate to them essential grace, for the natural head itself does not communicate essential

life to the members of the body *in act primo*; this comes rather from the soul as from the substantial form. The natural head communicates only some vital motion *in actu secundo.*" Garrigou-Lagrange, op. cit., 240.

⁵³ M. Corvez, O.P., who pleads for a simple return to old-time Thomism and a rejection of untenable compromises, openly declares that Christ *cannot* become the end or purpose of a pre-existent order, and that, therefore, the finality attributed to Christ by Thomists is a pseudo-finality. Christ can never be called the "end" of creation because the first production of beings was made independently of Him. Cf. art. cit., in *RTh* 49 (1949) 118. On this entire matter, cf. the important article by Bonnefoy, *La place du Christ dans le plan de la création*, in *MSR* 4 (1947) 257-284; 5 (1948) 39-62.

⁵⁴ E. Sauras, O.P., *El Cuerpo Místico de Cristo* (Madrid, 1952) c. 2, a. 2, p. 221.

⁵⁵ Sauras, op. cit., 228.

⁵⁶ Sauras, op. cit., 224.

⁵⁷ Sauras, op. cit., Ibid.

⁵⁸ Sauras, op. cit., 233-234.

⁵⁹ Sauras, op. cit., c. 4, a. 5, p. 710. In the second edition of his book (Madrid, 1956), Sauras has not changed his views on our subject.

⁶⁰ Cf. J. B. Carol, O.F.M., *The Aboslute Primacy . . .*, 147.

⁶¹ H. W. Schmidt, *Die Christusfrage. Beitrag zu einer christlichen Geschichtsphilosophie* (Gütersloh, 1929). See the long review by O. Holzer, O.F.M., *Hamartiozentrische oder christozentrische Theologie?* in *WuW* 6 (1939) 236-282; 7 (1940) 19-45.

⁶² O. Cullmann, *The Christology of the New Testament*, tr. Guthrie-Hall (Philadelphia, Pa., 1963); see the biblical index under: Rom. 8:29; Eph. 1:4; Col. 1:15-17. Cf. also his book, *Christ and Time*, tr. F. V. Filson (Philadelphia, Pa., 1964), under: Rom. 8:29; Eph. 1:4; and Col. 1:15-17.

⁶³ Cf. J. Gross, *La divinisation du chrétien d'après les Pères grecs* (Paris, 1939).

CHAPTER IV

¹ The treatise *De Incarnatione* was published in 1590 when Suárez was teaching theology at the University of Alcalá. It is found in volumes 17 and 18 of the *Opera omnia* edited by Vivès (Parisiis, 1856-66).

² For example, the important treatise *De Angelis*, found in volumes 2 and 3 of the Vivès edition, although it was published some thirty years after the *De Incarnatione*.

³ "Of the primary cause and reason for which the Incarnation was predestined and came to be, and without which it would not have come about." "For although God by a single and most simple act understands and wills all things, nonetheless since between knowledge and will, and among the things themselves which are

known or loved, there is a certain connection and dependence, in order to explain this we conceive certain things as being prior and posterior to others in the divine mind and will; in this way the prior and posterior are distinguished in these acts not according to the thing but according to reason. And explained in this way no theologian denies this order, and St. Thomas uses it often." Suárez, *De Incarnatione*, disp. V, sect 1, n. 1; ed. Vivès (Parisiis, 1860) XVII, 198.

[4] "God did not will this mystery only because the occasion of man's sin was offered as something foreknown, *but rather on the contrary*, sin was permitted so that from it He might take the occasion to communicate [Himself] to men in the most perfect way." Suárez, loc. cit., sect. II, n. 16; XVII, 223.

[5] Suárez, loc. cit., no. 18; XVII, 224-226.

[6] Suárez, loc. cit., sect. IV, n. 17; XVII, 244.

[7] St. Thomas holds that the grace of innocent Adam depended on Christ. Cf. *Summa theol.*, III, q. 1, a. 3, ad 5m; II-II, q. 2, a. 7. The grace of the Angels was also owed to Christ; cf. *Summa Theol.*, I, q. 57, a. 5, ad lm; q. 64, a. 1, ad 4m.

[8] Suárez, *De Angelis*, lib. VII, c. 13; ed. Vivès (Parisiis, 1856) II, 880-891.

[9] Suárez, *De Incarnatione*, disp. V, sect. III; XVII, 233ff.

[10] "Before the permission and proper and absolute prevision of sin, Christ was not predestined as Redeemer, but only after sin was permitted." Suárez, loc. cit., n. 11; XVII, 237-238.

[11] Suárez, *De Angelis*, lib. VI, c. 2.

[12] "Redeemer according to power, so to speak, and sufficiency [so that] his works might be most sufficient as a remedy, *if it were necessary*."Suárez, *De Incarnatione*, disp. V, sect. III, n. 11; XVII, 238.

[13] "No one is redeemed except he who is enslaved to sin." Suárez, loc. cit., sect. V; XVII, 251ff.

[14] "By absolute and efficacious will God willed the Incarnation only according to the substance of the mystery in this Person, in this individual nature; but He did not determine its mode until he permitted and foresaw sin."Suárez, *De Incarnatione*, disp. XLII, sect. II.

[15] "Nor is it enough that they were able to sin and were preserved by the merits of Christ. . . . This does not suffice for redemption properly understood, since redemption signifies a buying back." Suárez, Ibid.; cf. Risi, op. cit., I, 190.

[16] "They are not entirely proper and rigorous . . . ; but here we are explaining the proper and rigorous meaning of the words." Suárez, Ibid.

[17] " . . . grace is not given to the angels from the prevision of merits based on the death of Christ, but those based absolutely on the love and good works of the man Christ." Suárez, Ibid.

[18] "The sufficient and adequate motive for willing the Incarnation was not one, but many; not only partial, but total and sufficient *per se*." Suárez, *De Incarnatione*, disp. V, sect. 4, n. 7; XVII, 241.

[19] "The third opinion can be a middle one, which *in a certain way* embraces both [the Thomist and Scotist] positions; and it affirms the first reason for will-

ing this mystery to be both the excellence of the mystery itself as well as our redemption; so that in the first sign, by which God willed this mystery for both reasons, the divine will was inclined by a total motive." Suárez, loc. cit., n. 4; XVII, 239.

[20] Suárez, loc. cit., n. 21; XVII, 246.

[21] "In this controversy, considering the opinion which I have chosen and which I believe to be entirely true concerning the mode of the predestination of Christ, I hardly understand that there should be disagreement concerning the thing itself, though one might perhaps disagree with the manner of conceiving and explaining it." Suárez, loc. cit., sect. V; cf. Risi, op. cit., I, 200.

[22] Risi, op, cit., I, 201. To show the impossibililty of Suárez's theory, Fr. Chrysostome [Urrutibéhéty], op. cit., 334, calls our attention to the following axiom: "Un même effect ne saurait être le produit de deux causes totales adéquates; car alors l'effet dépendrait de chacune d'elles et n'en dépendrait pas. Il en dépendrait, puisque une cause n'est totale et adéquate qu'autant qu'elle produit son effet. Il n'en dépendrait pas, puisque l'une des causes cessant d'agir, l'autre produit l'effet."

[23] Cf. Risi, op. cit., 209.

[24] It is well known that Suárez's eclecticism depends, to a great extent, on his virtue of obedience to the directives of his Superiors.

[25] "I have never been able to assent to that opinion; and therefore I believe absolutely that, even had Adam not sinned, the Word would have taken human nature, although He would not have had the office of Redeemer." Suárez, *De Angelis*, lib. VII, c. 13, n. 9 (ed. Parisiis, 1856) II, 883-884.

CHAPTER V

[1] For further information on the contemporary Scotistic School, cf. the various publications of Father Bonnefoy, a truly outstanding scholar in this field. We mention particularly his often-cited *Il Primato di Cristo nella teologia contemporanea*, in *Problemi e Orientamenti di Teologia Dommatica* (Milano, 1957) II, 123-236.

[2] Further references in J. B. Carol, op. cit., 40-42.

[3] Risi, in his monumental work *Sul motivo della Incarnazione . . .* , frequently referred to above, explains at length the contribution of the Scotistic School.

[4] Cf. A. Sanna, O.F.M.Conv., *La regalità di Cristo secondo la Scuola franscescana* (Oristano, 1951); J.-F. Bonnefoy, O.F.M., *Un precurseur de la dévotion au Christ-Roi, Le T.R.P. Chrysostome Urrutibéhéty, O.F.M.*, in *SF* 8 (1936) 411-427; Fr. Chrysostome, O.F.M., *Doctrina et cultus Christi Regis in Ordine Fratrum Minorum*, in *Ant* 1 (1926) 289-308; Id., *La fête du Christ-Roi et le motif de l'Incarnation*, in *EF* 40 (1928) 459-480; 595-611; D. J. Unger, O.F.M.Cap., *A Prayer for Peace to the Prince of Peace*, in *ER* 104 (Jan.-June,

1941) 57-63; Id., *A Prayer to Christ the King*, in *AER* 107 (1942) 296-305.

[5] Cf. [Chrysostome Urrutibéhéty], *Christus Alpha et Omega, seu de Christi universali regno* (Lille, 1910); also the various articles by Unger and other authors mentioned in Carol, op. cit., 3-4.

[6] M. J. Scheeben, *The Mysteries of Christianity*, part IV, ch. XV, No. 64; tr. C. Vollert, S.J. (St. Louis, Mo., 1947) 419.

[7] "It conforms more to the judgement of [theological] reason," "it is more in conformity with the piety of faith, since it is more conformed to the authority of Scripture and the saints." Scheeben, loc. cit.

[8] Cf. U. Lattanzi, *Il Primato universale di Cristo secondo le Sacre Scritture* (Roma, 1937); Id., *Cristo nella gerarchia degli esseri secondo le Lettere della Cattività e quella ai Romani*, in *Dvts* 2 (1958) 472-485; Bonnefoy-Meilach, *Christ and the Cosmos* (Paterson, N.J., 1965); C. Burney, *Christ as the Arché of Creation: Prov. 8:22; Col. 1:15-18; Rev. 3:14*, in *JTS* 27 (1925-26) 160-177; Miguens, art. cit., in *ASCSI* III (Romae, 1968) 105-167.

[9] Scheeben, *The Mysteries* . . . , 430. On this cf. F. S. Pancheri, *Il pensiero di Scheeben e S. Tommaso* (Padova, 1965), ch. 1.

[10] Scheeben, op. cit., part X, ch. XXIX, No. 110; ed. cit., 795.

[11] St. Albert the Great, In III Sent., d. 20, a. 4.

[12] St. Bonaventure, In III Sent., d. 1, a. 2, q. 2; ed. cit. III, 23.

[13] St. Thomas, In III Sent., d. 1, a. 3. In the *Summa Theol.* he does not mention it.

[14] "But all of the authorities can be explained by saying that Christ would not have come as Redeemer unless man had fallen, *nor perhaps as possible*." Scotus, *Ordinatio*, III, d. 7, q. 3, ed. Balić, 5-6.

[15] This idea is current in theology. However, while it is very true that "to redeem" means to "free from sin," this notion is only partial and does not exhaust the complete meaning of redemption according to Sacred Scripture.

[16] Scotus himself had applied the concept of "preservative" redemption to our Blessed Lady.

[17] E.g., Peter Aureoli, Peter of Aquila, Rubió.

[18] Peter of Aquila, In III Sent., d. 2, q. 1 (ed. Venetiis, 1584) 328.

[19] Let us not forget that in Scotistic theology the two doctrines (i.e., the absolute primacy of Christ and Mary's Immaculate Conception) are always given parallel treatment. Hence it is legitimate to have one throw light on the other, as was always the case with our theologians.

[20] "Christ would have come as Redeemer; not as now in order to liberate from existing sin, but to preserve anyone from all sin whatever." William de Rubió (d. 1333), In III Sent., d. 20, q. 2 (ed. Parisiis, 1500) fol. 60r.

[21] St. Bernardine of Siena, *Sermo in feria sexta in Parasceve, art. 1 tertiae partis Dom. Passionis*. cap. 1 (ed. Ad Claras Aquas, 1956) V, 119-120.

[22] St. Bernardine, loc. cit.; V, 124-125.

[23] St. Bernardine is commenting on the famous text of St. Paul in Col. 1:19-20.

[24] St. Francis de Sales, *Treatise on the Love of God*, Book II, Ch. IV-V, tr. H. B. Mackey, O.S.B. (Westminster, Md., 1942) 73-78.

[25] For St. Lawrence's thought on the primacy, we have used particularly H. Borak, O.F.M.Cap., *Theologia historiae in doctrina S. Laurentii Brundusini*, in *Ltm* 1 (1960) 37-97; the best study on the subject is by Dominic of Herndon [Unger], O.F.M.Cap., *The Absolute Primacy of Christ Jesus and His Virgin Mother according To St. Lawrence of Brindisi*, in *CF* 22 (1952) 113-149. See also the scholarly article by B. Burkey, O.F.M.Cap., *The Theology of St. Joseph in the Writings of St. Lawrence of Brindisi*, in *CdJ* 16, No. 2 (1968) 263-292; 21, No. 1 (1973) 89-143, esp. 89-113, on the absolute primacy.

[26] St. Lawrence, *De Incarnationis mysterio ante omnia praedestinato*, in *Opera omnia* I: *Mariale* (Patavii, 1928) 19.

[27] St. Lawrence, *Explanatio in Genesim*; *Opera omnia*, III, 198-199.

[28] Cf. Borak, art. cit., 34.

[29] Cf. Borak, art. cit., 35ff.

[30] St. Lawrence, *Mariale*, 80-81.

[31] Cf. Borak, art. cit., 57-58. A good reason why Adam's sin could not have been foreseen before Christ is given by St. Lawrence as follows: "Nec satis capio quommodo in divina praescientia praevisio peccati Adae praecesserit Christi praedestinationem; nam praescientia peccati praesupponit praescientiam gratiae, sicut mors praesupponit vitam, infirmitas sanitatem, privatio omnis habitum. Et Adam prius fuit sanctus quam peccator. Peccatum originale privatio est gratiae et justitiae originalis; . . . Christus autem praedestinatus fuit fons totius gratiae et gloriae. Sic enim: Verbum caro factum est . . . Et de plenitudine ejus omnes nos acceptimus (Jo. 1:16)." *Mariale*, 81.

[32] M. J. Scheeben, *The Mysteries of Christianity*, tr. C. Vollert, S.J. (St. Louis, Mo. 1947); Id., *Handbuch der katholischen Dogmatik* (Freiburg i. B., 1882) III/1, 372 -377.

[33] Scheeben, *The Mysteries* . . . , part IV, Ch. XV, No. 64; Vollert ed., 423.

[34] Scheeben, op. cit., 424.

[35] Scheeben, op. cit., 424.

[36] Scheeben, Ibid.

[37] Scheeben, op. cit., 424-425.

[38] Scheeben, op. cit., 425.

[39] Scheeben, Ibid.

[40] Scheeben, op. cit., 427.

[41] Scheeben, loc. cit., No. 65; p. 431.

[42] Scotus, Opus Par., III, d. 7, q. 4; ed. Balić, 14-15.

[43] Scotus, In III Sent., d. 20, q. un.; ed. Vivès, XIV, 738.

[44] Scheeben, op. cit., Ch. XIV, No. 60, pp. 398-400.

[45] For the literature on Barth, let us mention only: H. U. von Balthasar, *K. Barth. Darstellung und Deutung seiner Theologie* (Köln, 1951); H. J. Iwand, *Vom Primat der Christologie*, in *Antwort: Karl Barth zum siebzigsten Geburtstag am 10. Mai 1956* (Zollinkon-Zürich, 1956) 172-189; J. de Senarchens, *La*

concentration christologique, ibid., 190-207; H. Bouillard, *Karl Barth: Genèse et évolution de la théologie dialectique* (Paris, 1957).

[46] The writings of Karl Barth are numerous; distributed through the span of several decades, they show the not-always-homogeneous evolution of his thought which had been marked as vigorous and well-structured ever since he published his *Römerbrief* in 1919.

[47] The volume has two parts: II/1 (Zürich, 1940) and II/2 (Zürich, 1942).

[48] K. Barth, *Kirchliche Dogmatik* (Zürich, 1942) II/2, 40-44.

[49] Barth, op. cit., II/2, 46-51.

[50] Barth, op. cit., II/1, 1-18.

[51] Barth, op. cit., 65ff.

[52] Barth, op. cit., II/2, 157. According to Barth, the Prologue of St. John's Gospel always speaks of the Word as *incarnandum* or as *incarnatum*. Recent exegetes are generally of the same opinion.

[53] Barth, op. cit., IV/1, 70. We have taken the text from the English version: *Church Dogmatics*, IV/1 (Edinburg, 1974) 66.

[54] We are referrring to the well-known text: "Incarnatio Christi non fuit occasionaliter praevisa; sed sicut finis immediate videbatur a Deo ab aeterno, ita Christus in natura humana, cum sit propinquior fini, caeteris prius praevidebatur, loquendo de his quae praedestinantur. Tunc iste ordo fuit in praevisione divina. Primo enim Deus intellexit se sub ratione Summi Boni, etc." Scotus, In III Sent., d. 19, q. un.

[55] Barth, op. cit., II/2, 154. In the English translation the whole discussion is found in II/2, 127-145.

[56] Barth, op. cit., IV/1, 48ff.

[57] This is the theme of the third volume of *Dogmatik*.

[58] Barth, op. cit., IV/1, 46ff.

[59] Scotus, *Ordinatio*, III, d. 3, q. 3; ed. Balić, 5.

[60] Cf. Bouillard, op. cit., 224ff.

CHAPTER VI

[1] There are no studies concerning the teaching of the Scotistic theologians of the post-Tridentine period. The following sources, however, throw some light (at least indirectly) on the subject: J. H. Sbaralea, O.F.M.Conv., *Supplementum et castigatio ad Scriptores Trium Ordinum S. Francisci a Waddingo aliisque descriptos*, 3 vols. (Romae, 1908-1936); G. Franchini, O.F.M.Conv., *Bibliosofia e Memorie letterarie di scrittori francescani che hanno scritto dopo il 1585* (Modena, 1693); G. Brotto-G. Zonta, *La facoltà teologica dell'Università di Padova*, I (Padova, 1922); D. Scaramuzzi, O.F.M., *Il pensiero di Giovanni Duns Scoto nel Mezzogiorno d'Italia* (Roma, 1927); Id., *Lo Scotismo nell'Università e nei Collegi di Roma* (Roma, 1939); Dominique de Caylus, O.F.M.Cap., *Merveilleux épanoissement de l'Ecole scotiste au XVIIe siècle*, in *EF* 24 (1910)

5-21; 493-502; 25 (1911) 35-47; 300-307; 627-645; 26 (1912) 276-288; N. Papini, O.F.M.Conv., *Lectores publici O.F.M.Conv. a saec. XIII ad saec, XIX*, posthumous work, published in *MF* 31 (1931) 95-102; 170-174; 259-260; 32 (1932) 33-36; 72-77; 33 (1933) 67-74; 242-261.

[2] Fabbri (1564-1630) is the great pioneer of the flourishing Scotistic movement in the post-Tridentine period. On his many talents, cf. Franchini, op. cit., 205.

[3] Philippus Faber, O.F.M.Conv., *Disputationes Theologicae in III Librum Sent. complectentes materiam de Incarnatione*, dist. 7. q. 3, disp. 19, n. 1ff. Cf. St. Thomas, *Summa Theol.*, I, q. 23, a. 5; St. Bonaventure, In I Sent., d. 40; In III Sent., d. 11, a. 1; Scotus, In III Sent., d. 7, q. 3, n. 2.

[4] Faber, op. cit., disp. 20, n. 1 (ed. Venetiis, 1613) 103. Apparently, Faber is not aware of Suárez's "Tertia via."

[5] ". . . with many reasons, yet he declares that he affirms without prejudice; for Scotus especially among the Scholastics always uses the greatest moderation." Faber, op. cit., loc. cit., n. 8; ed. cit., 104.

[6] St. Thomas, *Summa Theol.*, I. q. 23, a. 5.

[7] Faber, loc. cit., nn. 9-21; ed. cit., 104-108.

[8] "However, this reply [of Cajetan] does not answer the argument. For this proposition [Scotus' axiom] bears its own proof: for he says, 'The one who wills ordinately,' and not, 'The one who wills absolutely.' Whenever, therefore, there is a free agent who freely wills several things in an ordered way, that is, according as those things are desirable and among them some are more desirable than others, the will first and mostly desires that which *in itself* is first and more desirable, before that which is less desirable *in itself.* Otherwise the will would not be ordered, just as one who loves the body more than the soul does not will in an ordered manner. That major premise is therefore true *simpliciter* both on the level of the possible and of the actual in an ordered will." Faber, loc. cit., n. 22; ed. cit., 108.

[9] Faber, borrowing from Scotus, shows some of the untenable consequences that follow from the Thomistic thesis, for example, that Christ would have to rejoice over Adam's sin because without it He would not have existed.

[10] Faber, loc. cit., n. 28-33; ed. cit., 110-111.

[11] Faber, loc. cit., n. 32; ed. cit., 111.

[12] Faber, loc. cit., n. 34; ibid.

[13] Faber, disp. 48, n. 7.

[14] B. Bellutus, *Disputationes de Incarnatione* . . . , disp. 7, q. 2, n. 33 (Cataniae, 1645) 106-107.

[15] Bellutus, loc. cit., nn. 34-39; ed. cit., 107-108.

[16] Bellutus, loc. cit., n. 50; ed. cit., 110.

[17] "Before the foreknowledge of sin Christ was not chosen as Redeemer." Bellutus, loc. cit., n. 54; ed. cit., 111.

[18] Bellutus, loc. cit., n. 55; ibid.

[19] Bellutus, loc. cit., n. 56; ibid.

[20] Bellutus, disp. 8. q. 2; ed. cit., 145.

[21] Bellutus, loc. cit., n. 20; ibid.

[22] "The true exemplar after the likeness of which God predestined the rest of the elect." Bellutus, loc. cit., n. 21; ed. cit., 145-146.

[23] Bellutus, loc. cit., n. 23; ed. cit., 146.

[24] He is referring to Suárez's comment on the Third Part of the *Summa Theol* of St. Thomas, disp. 41, and in the tract *De praedestinatione*, c. 24. He is followed by several other theologians, including the Scotist Angelo Volpi [Vulpes] who wrote a lengthy commentary on Scotus—12 volumes in folio (Naples, 1622-1646).

[25] "I affirm, however, that Christ did not merit for us the first predestination and election to glory, even because of [His] love." Bellutus, op. cit., disp. 13, q. 2, n. 58.

[26] Bellutus, ibid.

[27] Bellutus, loc. cit., n. 73.

[28] Bellutus, loc. cit., n. 75.

[29] Bellutus, Ibid.

[30] " . . . since He preserved them not from any sin which they would necessarily have incurred, but from a sin which they could commit on account of their freedom." Bellutus, loc. cit., n. 76.

[31] Bellutus, loc. cit., q. 4. n. 77; disp. 16, q. 2, n. 40.

[32] Mastri's philosophical works—five bulky tomes in folio—(Venice, 1678) were held in high esteem and had many editions during the seventeenth and eighteenth centuries. Some of them were written in collaboration with his friend Belluti while they were teaching together in Padua.

[33] The title of the work is: *Disputationes Theologicae in III Librum Sententiarum* . . . (ed. Venetiis, 1719); first edition: 1661.

[34] "This is the most celebrated controversy among all those concerning the third part [of the *Summa*] or third Book of the Sentences." Mastrius, *Disputationes* . . . , disp. 4, q. 1, n. 1 (ed. Venetiis, 1719) 206.

[35] G. Hurtado, S.J., *De Incarnatione Verbi* (Alcalá, 1628); D. Granado, S.J., *Comment. in III Partem Summae* (Granatae, 1633); R. Aversa a Sanseverino, Cl. Reg. Min., *Sacrae Theologiae tertia pars in qua de Deo Incarnato* . . . (Genuae, 1640). The authors cited in favor of the Thomistic and Scotistic theses are numerous; among the Thomists: Cajetan, Medina, Capreolus, Ferrariensis, Molina, Valencia, Vázquez, Becanus, Bonacina, Curiel, Lugo, Bernal, Amicus, Arriaga, Cornejo, Ragusa, Tanner, Orlandus, Meracius, Pasqualigo, Caspensis. For the Scotistic thesis: Tataretus, Lichetus, Mayronis, Fabbri, Rada, Volpi, Belluti, Ponce, Gallo, Aretinus, Centini, Baldi, Morandi, Aresio.

[36] Mastrius, op. cit., disp. 4, q. 1, n. 2; ed. cit., 206.

[37] Mastrius, loc. cit., a. 4, n. 4; ed. cit., 207.

[38] " . . . otherwise the natural son would be loved for the sake of the servant and in dependence upon the love of servants." Mastrius, loc. cit., a. 3, n. 45; ed. cit., 214.

[39] " . . . which, however, are very diverse, so that what is prior in one is posterior in the other." Mastrius, loc. cit., a. 1, n. 15; ed. cit., 209.

[40] J. de Rada, O.F.M., *Controversiae Theologicae inter S. Thomam et Scotum, in III Sent.*, controv. V, a. 3 (ed. Coloniae Agrippinae, 1620) III, 165.

[41] Mastrius, op. cit., disp. 4, q. 1, a. 3, n. 47; ed. cit., 214.

[42] "First God understood Himself as the first Good. . . . Thirdly, willing the manifestation of His goodness, etc." Mastrius, loc. cit., a. 1, n. 13; ed. cit., 208..

[43] Mastrius, loc. cit., a. 5, n. 73; ed. cit., 219-220.

[44] "Christ was not first predestined as Redeemer." Mastrius, loc. cit., a. 2, n. 22; ed. cit., 210.

[45] "The Incarnation is worthy of love on its own account as the end of the other works of God; the passion and death of Christ not on their own account but as a remedy for sin and as a means of restoration." Mastrius, loc. cit., n. 28; ed. cit., 211.

[46] " . . . that Christ might have something to cure through His Passion." Mastrius, loc. cit., n. 26; ed. cit., 210.

[47] Mastrius, Ibid.

[48] Mastrius, loc. cit., n. 30; ed. cit., 211.

[49] " . . . in the universal but in the particular; otherwise the act of willing would not be efficacious." Mastrius, loc. cit., n. 34; ed. cit., 212.

[50] Ibid.

[51] " . . . only virtually and *in causa* but not formally and in itself." Mastrius, loc. cit., n. 35; ed. cit., 212.

[52] Mastrius, loc. cit., n. 36; ed. cit., 212.

[53] Mastrius, loc. cit., a. 5. n. 65; ed. cit., 218. Cf. G. Vázquez, *In III Partem Summae*, q. 1. a. 3, disp. X, c. VI (ed. Lugduni, 1631) 84.

[54] Mastrius, loc. cit., nn. 67-72; ed. cit., 218-219.

[55] " . . . as for an end that was total and more principally loved; for they say that this end [i.e., the one more principally loved] is Christ's own glory and exaltation. Therefore, that end was not the redemption alone." Mastrius, loc. cit., a. 4, n. 58; ed. cit., 216.

[56] Mastrius, op. cit., disp. 3, q. 13, a. 2.

[57] Mastrius, loc. cit., nn. 487-488.

[58] Mastrius, loc. cit., n. 489.

[59] Mastrius, loc, cit., n. 492.

[60] "Implies a greater excellence in Christ our Lord." Mastrius, loc. cit., n. 493.

[61] "For when it comes to honoring Christ, I rather overdo it than fall short of the praise due to Him, if owing to my ignorance I should have to succumb to either alternative." Scotus, *Ordinatio*, III, d. 13, q. 4; ed. Vivès, XIV, 463; cf. Mastrius, op. cit., disp. 4, a. 7, n. 8.

CHAPTER VII

¹Blaise Pascal (d. 1662), *Thoughts*, n. 548; tr. W. F. Trotter, in *Harvard Classics* (New York, 1910) XLVIII, 177.

² K. Barth, *Dogmatics in Outline*, tr. G. T. Thomas (SCM Press, London, 1958) 66.

³ "One must begin from the center, which is Christ." St. Bonaventure, *In Hexaëmeron; Op. omn.* V, 330.

⁴ "Christ is the one Teacher of all." This is the title of a famous lecture by the Seraphic Doctor. Cf. *Op. omn.* V, 367-574.

⁵ J. A. Möhler, *Symbolik, oder Darstellung der dogmatischen Gegensätze der Katholiken und Protestanten nach ihren öffentlichen Bekenntnisschriften* (Mainz, 1832) No. 48.

⁶ Cf. H. Hernández Cirre, O.F.M. Cap., *El primado unversal de Cristo a la luz del Vaticano II*, in *EstF* 69 (1968) 5-40.

⁷ G. Marcel, *Être et avenir* (Paris, 1935) 196-197.

⁸ Cf. *Informations catholiques internationales*, n. 132 (1960) 14.

⁹ On the inadequate treatment of the doctrine of creation in our theology textbooks, see M. Flick-Z. Alszeghy, *Il Creatore* (Firenze, 1959), *Introduction*.

¹⁰ Cf. L. Cerfaux, *Christ in the Theology of St. Paul*, tr. Webb-Walker (New York, 1959) 429-432; H. Schlier, *Der Brief an die Epheser* (Düsseldorf, 1957); J. Sittler (Lutheran), *Called to Unity*, in *EmR* 14 (1962) 177-187; O. Cullmann, *Christ and Time* (Philadelphia, 1964), bibl. index under Col. 1:15-18.

INDEX OF AUTHORS